A SCORNED WOMAN

WOMAN

The Queen

This book is a work of fiction. Names, characters, places, and incident are the product of the author's imagination or are used fictitiously. Any resemblance to actual events or locales or persons, living or dead, is entirely coincidental.

ISBN-13: 978-0-9827-2239-8
ISBN-10: 0-9827-2239-X

For information regarding special ordering for bulk purchases, contact:
Queendom Dreams Publishing - www.queendomdreamspublishing.com

Queendom Dreams Publishing

ACKNOWLEDGEMENTS

As always, I give all honor and thanks unto Jehovah God. For without His grace, no talent that I have been blessed with would come to fruition. I thank Him for the past, present, and the blessings to come.

Extra special thanks to YOU, my supporters and friends of The Queen. Words will never express the level of gratitude I have for you. Without you, I am just another person writing books. Prayerfully, you will stick with me along my journey and inspire me to want to give you more. It's because of you that I continue to press along this difficult road. It's because of your prayers and words of encouragement to "Never give up," that I keep picking up the pen. Continue to spread the word.

The Queen

A SCORNED WOMAN

The Queen

Queendom Dreams Publishing

www.QueendomDreamsPublishing.com

1

Michelle, I really think you're making a big mistake. You are rushing into this marriage and you don't know crap about this man."

Michelle twirled around in her seat at the vanity table with disbelief written on her freshly made-up face. "On my wedding day? Really, Angie? Must we go there today? You said you would support my decision, and here you are again with this nonsense."

Angie paced back and forth in the large bridal suite and then stopped to meet Michelle's piercing eyes. "I'm having a difficult time watching you about to make the biggest mistake of your life. We've been best friends for twelve years, and I've sat and watched some real jerks come and go in your life, but it was okay because you weren't marrying any of them or throwing away your life with them. You got wise, picked yourself up, and kept it moving—"

Michelle slammed her petite, delicate hand on the vanity table. She had been frustrated with the dating scene for a while. Although her friend from college had a valid point about not knowing much about her groom-to-be, Calvin Edwards, none of the others ever proposed marriage to her. Michelle's previous boyfriend of five years only ended the relationship when the woman he cheated with became pregnant and he *needed* to marry her because it was "the right thing to do." But there was never a thought or discussion about marrying Michelle.

Michelle's position as a talk show host on the *Michelle Post Love & Lies Show* caused her to engage a public relations firm when her ex's new wife called in on a live broadcast and lied to the world about Michelle trying to fight her when it came out that she was pregnant and was about to marry their mutual boyfriend, Tony. Although the words were bogus, it tarnished Michelle's squeaky-clean reputation and exposed that she had her own out-of-control drama while she gave advice to everyone else.

Michelle spotted Calvin when she entered the PR firm where he worked. She was immediately drawn to the bulging biceps that protruded in his Dolce & Gabbana dress shirt. She was disappointed when he walked by her, barely acknowledging her presence. She could immediately tell that he had an important position because the workers in the vicinity seemed to tighten up as he breezed past.

Taking a page from her own book of advice on love, she boldly asked if she could meet the six-two Adonis after her meeting with her PR agent. When Calvin entered the office, the scent of his cologne filled her nostrils, and his thick lips caused a quiver between her legs. Once again her feelings were crushed by his detached demeanor and the way he seemed to look through her and not at her.

Michelle knew she was a solid, attractive woman at five-two, and typically she could turn any man's head. She deduced Calvin to be gay since he didn't seem the least bit interested in her. She had already surveyed his large hand for the presence of a wedding band, but there was none.

Two weeks later, when Calvin called her to invite her out for dinner, she discarded her notion of him being gay. He apologized for being so short with her while at the firm and explained that he was striving to make partner in the dog-eat-dog atmosphere.

Calvin wined and dined Michelle every night for two weeks, and he never made an attempt to sleep with her. It had been over a year since she'd been touched by a man, so she was anticipating a chance to jump his bones. By their third week of dating, Michelle threw caution to the wind and invited him back to her home after their date. He refused her and told her he wanted to hold out for his wife. Michelle was disappointed again, but she admired him for not being a dog.

When he proposed the following week, Michelle's raging hormones answered "yes" for her. She was a bit apprehensive about not really knowing anything about his life beyond what he told her, but she was already behind schedule in her grand scheme of life to be married by the age of thirty and having her first child at thirty-one. She was already thirty-one, and Calvin seemed like her first chance at a committed boyfriend, let alone a husband. Although all sorts of men hit on Michelle, they'd always fall below her standards, and she wouldn't give them the time of day.

At times, Michelle envied her best friend. Angie had a child at seventeen but then declared herself a lesbian in her mid-twenties, although she experimented prior to then. Michelle loved the bond that Angie had with her son, Romeo, and she often wished she had her own child to have the same bond with. Angie was always dedicated to whatever she set out to do despite having a child and being on her own at a young age. It was how they met. Angie had an off-campus apartment and advertised for a roommate, as she juggled a full load at school, a full-time job, and her son. Michelle wasn't thrilled about the idea of rooming with a single mother, but sharing a dorm room with three other temperamental girls made an occasional crying baby more appealing.

With Angie having a broadcasting background and Michelle having a journalism background, Angie put the wheels in motion to start Michelle's talk show, which became quite successful and had been running for close to three years on television and three years on the internet. Everything was going well until the snag with the Tony's baby momma.

"Would you stop it, please?" Michelle yelled with tears forming in her eyes. "I'm getting married today. I am not throwing my life away. I am not making any mistakes. I want a family, and now I will have a family. My mother and grandmother are happy for me. Why can't you be happy too? I have a wonderful, handsome, successful man who is ambitious and he wants to marry me of all people. Do you know how many women shamelessly try to throw themselves at him?"

"Like you did when we met him just five months ago?" Angie tried to contain her laughter in the serious moment.

"Whatever! I didn't throw myself at him. I just asked to meet him." She turned her head back toward the vanity mirror and pretended to smooth her already perfect hair, not wanting Angie to see the guilt in her eyes.

Angie walked up behind Michelle and looked at her darting eyes through the mirror. "I was there, Michelle. Remember? You got all upset because he didn't pay any attention to your bulging cleavage after you undid that top button to your blouse. You even accused the man of being gay and said that I should know just because I'm a lesbian. I don't care what you say. Marriage or no marriage, I think his ass is suspect." She chuckled.

She turned back to face her friend. "Why, because he chose to wait for marriage to have sex? That's just ridiculous. I would think he'd be suspect if he wasn't pressing for a quick wedding. He obviously can't wait to get to the goodies." Michelle also chuckled at the thought despite her growing anger toward her friend. "And he knows I want children as soon as possible, which makes him even better suited for me."

"That doesn't mean anything. He could be a down-low child molester for all you know."

Michelle turned away from Angie again, this time avoiding the mirror. She didn't want Angie to read her eyes and see that she had wondered herself if Calvin was one of those down-low men or even a child molester. She would be the laughingstock of Atlanta if she married one after dishing out all the things to watch out for to her millions of viewers on her very own show. But then she concluded that you could never really tell these things with any man.

Michelle and her older sister, Milara, were molested by their grandfather. Michelle lived in denial about it until she began therapy at thirteen after Milara killed their grandfather and herself when she turned sixteen. She left a note speaking of the molestation endured each summer they'd visit their grandparents. Michelle's grandfather was a well-respected preacher with his own church in Savannah, Georgia. After the deaths, Michelle's mother confessed to also being abused by her father, leading to her decision to never marry. She was content with having two daughters out of wedlock.

Michelle didn't want to go through life so untrusting and unable to love, so she channeled her energy into creating a talk show to promote trust and love. She was glad she kept her personal love life out of the public eye. It was humiliating enough to be dumped by a man who wasted five years of her life without a commitment, but having the world know that she didn't have a clue about love would be far more devastating. That was the reason she became desperate for help with her public image after Tony's baby momma called in to the show.

Michelle had convinced herself that Calvin had to be God-sent because of the timing and his firm preference to abstain from premarital sex. She also appreciated that Calvin's salary was three times greater than her six-figure salary, which she formerly shared with Tony, who wanted to be an entrepreneur without any real business plan. Michelle supported all of his business ventures because her philosophy was that black women needed to be more supportive of their black men in order to hold onto them. The fact that he cheated on her wasn't a hard pill to swallow because she wanted to be open-minded in their relationship to keep from pushing him away. When Tony's new woman called into the show and identified herself as Caucasian, Michelle was made angrier by the fact that she was abandoned for a white woman than she was by the content of the phone call.

Michelle hadn't been with Tony the fourteen months prior to the crazy woman's call and couldn't understand why the woman suddenly decided to attack her without provocation. Angie had long ago suggested that Tony was probably laid up with another woman on Michelle's dime, but Michelle blew that notion off, bragging that she knew how to take care of her man. For the longest Michelle didn't know why Tony would never move into the

2,700-square-foot home she had built in Conyers. Instead, he chose to stay in his small, shabby home in Decatur that wasn't in a good neighborhood, because he was trying to get a music studio together. After the place was robbed twice, he still remained, and Michelle helped him to rebuild each time because that's what got him out of his funk, which put a damper on their sex life.

Angie had a problem with every guy Michelle dated. Michelle always pegged Angie's warnings as jealousy because of the brief and experimental romance she and Angie shared during their college years. Despite the experiment, the pair decided it was best to just be friends and went back to dating men. After a couple of years of bisexual relationships, Angie declared herself 100 percent lesbian.

At times Michelle found herself a bit jealous when she'd meet some of the beautiful women Angie dated. Being a gay woman didn't fit into Michelle's grand scheme of life, though, so she focused on snagging a man she could marry and have plenty of children with. Calvin Edwards fit perfectly in her plan. He was only thirty-three, an aspiring partner at the PR firm where he had worked for seven years, and he owned a fabulous Mediterranean-style six-bedroom, seven-bath, four-million-dollar house in Buckhead. Compared to a thirty-six-year-old Tony, Calvin was definitely a man with a plan. Michelle just hoped Calvin could measure up to Tony in the bedroom. She still masturbated to the wonderful memories of Tony's sex game. She figured she'd find out soon enough, as the knock at the door of the bridal suite let them know the wedding was ready to begin.

Angie stood near her with her arms crossed. "I still think you're making a big mistake. There's something sneaky as hell about this man. I just can't put my finger on it yet."

"I love you too, Angie, now drop it!" Michelle said, ushering her Maid of Honor to the door.

2

don't see what the big rush is. You have known this woman all of five minutes."

Calvin stopped fixing his tie and turned from the mirror in disgust and looked over at his unenthused best man relaxing on the chaise lounge in the groom's suite with one leg propped up. "David, stop it. I'm getting married today. Anyway, I thought you said you liked Michelle."

"I do. She's hot, and a career woman is a plus—but marriage? Atlanta has too many available women for you to consider. You're still young," David responded, toying with his cufflinks.

"And I'm trying to make partner while I'm still young. I need to present a stable front." Calvin walked over to the large window to gaze out as the thought of soon becoming partner brought a crooked smile upon his face.

"A front? A front?" David asked, shooting up from his seat with a look of shock on his face. "You're messing with this girl's head because you're trying to impress people to become a partner? What the hell happened to love? Damn, I expected you to profess your undying love for the girl, but you're talking about some damn partnership. Hell, I want partnership too, but you don't see me running off to get married to anyone."

Calvin rushed to David. "Calm down," he said in a whisper. "I'm not just marrying her for that. I do like her. I think she's the ideal type of woman to marry, so what's the point in waiting? If she's right, she's right. I think it'll be pretty cool to have a wife to come home to every night. I have that big house and I'd like to fill it with kids one day. So does Michelle. Most of these women are not willing to trade in their careers for family. I figure if I get this partnership, I'll make more money and can have all the children I can afford. Tell me, what or who should I hold out longer for? If I could start my family right away, why shouldn't I?" Calvin stood before David with a reassuring hand on each shoulder.

David shook his head. While Calvin made some valid points, he never heard him mention that he was in love with Michelle. He also didn't like the idea of people bringing children into a situation without knowing if the marriage is a good fit or not. He especially didn't like that Calvin was marrying Michelle when David saw her the day she and Angie came to the firm and he let Calvin know that he wanted to meet Michelle for himself. Calvin kept promising David that he'd get Michelle's contact information and set the two of them up. Instead, just a few weeks later, Calvin blindsided him with a wedding announcement. Now, only four months after that announcement, the two were getting married. He even thought her friend Angie was fine as hell, but she made no qualms about being gay.

"I just think maybe you oughta wait a year or two. Even wait a year before starting with the kids. Just to be sure she's the right one. You don't want to be clocking partner salary and she ends up with half of it as child support."

"See, it's that type of thinking that will keep you from ever being a partner at the firm. You're too negative and you can't see the big picture. You need to learn to be more of an optimist like myself. I believe my marriage will be prosperous and fruitful, and Michelle will be just as happy as I." He animated his hands in the air as to create a visual picture for David to see.

"Do you love her, Calvin? Do you even love her?" David asked, frustrated.

Calvin put his hand on David's shoulder again. "David, David, David. Back in the old days, people didn't marry for love. Half the time they hadn't even seen the person they were going to marry. Those people remained married into their ripe old age. Now everyone is on this 'I love you' trip, then they run to the altar and then to the divorce court a month later. Would it be better if I just have casual sex with Michelle, get her pregnant, and still don't marry her because we aren't in love? I mean, where's the glory in that? It happens every day. Look at your situation. You would know.

"Michelle wants to be married and so do I. Michelle wants to have plenty of children and so do I. Michelle understands the important things that it takes to make a successful relationship, and that means to 'support your man and he will take care of his woman.' She wants me to make partner. She understands that my having a stable front will in turn benefit her. We're both getting what we want and need, but right now I just need for you to support me on my decision. I know you wanted Michelle yourself, but you have to admit, you two are not as compatible as she and I. You're not trying to be married and you already have a ten-year-old daughter—and might I add, you never married the mother of."

David pulled away from Calvin to pour himself a glass of water from the suite's wet bar. "I am thankful for my daughter, but that is why I feel strongly against bringing children into an equation that may not work. I still go through hell to see my daughter. I just don't want you to have to go through the same."

David held up an empty glass to offer Calvin, but he held up a hand to decline.

"David, we've been good friends for like seven years now, right?"

David thought and then nodded.

"To be quite honest, you're like the best friend I've ever had in my life," Calvin continued as David smiled, touched by the words. "Think about all the women that you know and tell me if you could think of one woman that even comes close to Michelle."

David thought again as he swallowed his water and shrugged his shoulders when he couldn't think of a single woman in Michelle's league.

"That's exactly my point. This is why I see no point in waiting to marry her. I don't need to wait and see if I'll lose her. I asked her to marry me, she said yes, we set a date, and today is that day. Please be happy for me. For us. I've caught enough hell from my own family about this, but at least they've come to accept my decision and have embraced my wife-to-be. I just need my best friend to get on board, especially since he's my best man."

David reluctantly agreed, holding out his hand to shake Calvin's before embracing. The knock at the door signaled that the time had come for the wedding to begin.

3

Calvin

The officiate pronounced Calvin and Michelle husband and wife before the crowded church. There were at least five hundred guests on the inside, and many of Michelle's fans had camped outside to witness the union. The newlyweds made their way to the foyer in the back of the sanctuary. As they approached the last row of pews, Calvin's heartbeat sped up as his eyes locked with the unforgettable blue eyes of the brunette. His smile became plastered as his heart raced, anticipating Julissa's fiery and unpredictable personality that had often turned him on. Her mere presence made him sweat, both from the thought of her causing a scene before the hundreds of guests and from the excitement she brought to his loins. He was glad when the picture taking ended and he could escape her piercing eyes. Had it been up to him, Julissa would have been the one standing at his side, but making partner meant more to him than love. As much as he loved Julissa, he knew she'd never be accepted by his family and friends.

The only thing predictable about Julissa was that she'd always do something unpredictable. She was a high-fashion catalogue and runway model and was introduced to Calvin through a client three years prior. Temperamental was a mild word to describe her. She hated the fact that Calvin kept their relationship a secret. She also hated when Calvin's firm took their top performers and their mates to Aruba a year ago, and he took a different white woman as his date. Julissa flew to Aruba just to let Calvin have it. She calmed down when he snuck off to have sex with her.

Julissa wanted Calvin to get that partnership and would rally to help him gain big-time, international clients for his portfolio. She didn't like when Calvin told her the senior partners were riding him for not being a family-man, as they were, and not presenting the right image needed to be a partner. Because the firm only employed a handful of black men and each of them were striving for the same prize of being the token black male partner and joining the three black women and six white partners. Julissa accepted the charade that Calvin needed to play in order to win.

Calvin looked up after taking pictures with his new bride and their families to see where Julissa had gotten off to.

"Who are you looking for, honey?" Michelle asked, when Calvin's neck stretched. It was obvious he was looking for someone.

"Oh, no one. I was just looking to see if we're going to be able to sneak out of here so I could be with my new wife," he purred seductively.

Michelle playfully tapped him and smiled a big blushing smile. "Ooh, you're so bad. I like, I like." She reached up and kissed her husband again as Calvin's eyes scanned the sanctuary to see if Julissa was somewhere watching. He hoped she'd just go home, but it would be so unlike her.

"Get a room, you two!" Angie yelled out at the kissing couple, while the remaining crowd laughed.

When Calvin and Michelle broke apart, someone said, "We better get them to the reception so they can go home." Again the small crowd laughed.

Only minutes after the bride and groom made their grand entrance into the reception hall at the Grand Hyatt in Buckhead, there were sounds of awe as Julissa made her own grand entrance with a date. She had gone to her rented suite at the hotel to change into a dress that made the bride's dress look like something you'd wear to a junior-high formal. The guests oohed and ahhed at the spectacular gown. Calvin had relaxed the entire fifteen minutes he didn't see Julissa at the reception. Once he saw her, a combination of fear and anger took hold of him. His fear was because he didn't know what she would do, and the anger was because Julissa had a handsome, well-built date.

"Oh no that bitch didn't come in here trying to outdo me on my wedding day. Do you know her?" Michelle asked Calvin. "A disgruntled ex maybe?"

From the head table, Calvin squinted, pretending to try getting a good look. "She looks like a woman I represented a few years back. She's a high-fashion model or something."

"Did you invite her?"

"No. Maybe she heard about the wedding on the news or something. I was surprised so many of your fans were waiting outside of the church to see you."

Michelle smiled, accepting that. "Yeah, that was crazy. But I think my handsome husband has his own nutty fan club," she said, looking at Julissa signing autographs in the middle of the dance floor. "I ought to go give her a piece of my mind. Why would she come in here with that Cinderella gown on as if she's trying to steal my thunder?"

Calvin kissed Michelle to prevent her from getting up to approach Julissa. "Don't worry about her, baby. This is your day—our day—and she can't undo what we have. Don't let her get to you. As I recall, that's just her normal personality. I remember her being hard to control, if that's the same person."

Michelle kissed Calvin again, keeping one eye on Julissa. "You're right, this is our day."

Calvin felt his blood curdle when he saw Julissa kissing her date as if they were the newlyweds.

"Well, at least she's got her own man, so I'm not going to think any more about her. She's pretty, though. Maybe Angie will try to holler at her the minute her boyfriend turns his back." Michelle laughed, further pissing Calvin off.

As the festivities continued, Julissa made her way around the large room grander than the bride. Unbeknownst to Michelle, many people told Julissa how she accomplished the mission she set out to do, which was making the bride's dress look subpar and giving the appearance that she was in love with her rented date. When Julissa came out of the ladies' room, she saw Calvin standing there tight-jawed, waiting for her.

"Let's go!" he commanded under his breath to keep others from hearing. The two walked down the hall as curious eyes followed. "What the hell do you think you're doing?" he asked, trying to hide his anger as they walked.

"What? I just wanted to see the man I love leave me for a fishy-bitch and get married to make his employers happy."

"Stop it! I was just with you last night. You know what this marriage is all about. You know I only love you and not her, so stop with the damn games."

"Calm down, sweetie. People are going to think we're arguing," Julissa said, playfully laughing for the onlookers. "You're the one playing games with this marriage. Now I'm supposed to be okay while you put my big, black, delicious cock up inside of that smelly tramp? And then I'm supposed to wait two weeks for you to return with the bitch from your honeymoon and you won't even tell me where you're going?"

"You're making me regret telling you where my wedding was at. Now go home! I will see you before I leave. Promise. But if you don't leave right now and lose that bozo you brought with you, you won't see me."

Julissa was so excited and wanted to jump up and kiss Calvin right in the hall in front of everyone, but she had to contain herself. "Really?"

"Yes, really. Now go on and get out of here." Calvin looked around to see who all was looking and quietly said, "I love you."

"I love you too, my chocolate god."

Calvin smiled. He loved when Julissa would refer to him as her "chocolate god." It made him feel mightier in the bed. He watched as Julissa walked away without going back to the banquet room for her date. As Calvin turned to walk back to the ballroom, he saw David leaning up against the wall watching, obviously expecting an explanation.

4

Michelle

Where did that husband of yours get off to, Shelly?" Michelle's seventy-five-year-old grandmother asked. "I want him to dance with me."

"He went to use the men's room, Grandma. He'll be right back."

"They're playing all this good music. I want to dance. He promised me a dance."

"He's coming, Grandma," Michelle repeated while wondering where he had gotten off to. Cinderella had also disappeared, and Michelle noticed her date sitting alone and looking like a fish out of water.

"I saw him walking down the hall with the Snow White chick wearing the big dress. Bitch reminds me of the good witch from the Wizard of Oz, without any good though," Angie snarled. "What's up with that, Michelle? An ex-girlfriend maybe?"

"That's not an ex-girlfriend," Michelle defended. She took a few steps away to keep her grandmother from hearing. "That's one of his clients, for your information. She's a high-fashion model. He said she's one of those out-of-control clients who does everything impulsively. I'm sure he just went to thank her for coming."

Angie looked at Michelle, hoping she wasn't as stupid as she sounded. "And she couldn't speak to you, why?"

"I didn't want to meet her," Michelle said, looking away from Angie's suspicious eyes. "He knew I wanted to give her a piece of my mind for coming here in that dress."

"Yeah, whatever! If you weren't having this shotgun wedding, you could have taken the time to get that perfect wedding gown, as you always dreamed."

"I'm fine with my dress." Michelle's voice raised an octave higher, further indicating her deception. "This is my dream wedding."

"If you say so," Angie said, holding her hand up. She was disgusted with Michelle's naivety. "I'm going to find me a drink," she said before walking away.

Before Calvin returned a whole twenty minutes after that, Michelle tried to hide her anger from the droves of people coming to ask her where her groom was at. She couldn't say, because she didn't know herself.

Calvin came up behind Michelle, kissing her on the side of her face. "Please don't kill me. I was being pulled by one person after the other and I didn't want to seem rude to our guests."

Michelle smiled, reassured by the warmth she felt in his embrace. "I understand. I thought I was going to have to start fighting for my husband already."

"Trust me. You'll never have to fight for me. I know who my wife is and I know where home is at." He kissed her again, this time catching her lips when she turned her head for him. "How much longer do we have to be here? I'm ready to get out of here."

"I don't know. This is my first wedding . . ."

"And only wedding," Calvin added.

Michelle smiled, in love with the thought. "That too. I know my grandma is waiting for her dance, so I think you better get out there and cut a rug if you're trying to leave anytime soon." She chuckled.

Calvin laughed. "Your grandma isn't going to hurt me, is she? She looks like she can put a hurting on a brother out on the dance floor."

"Just tell her to take it easy on you. She will."

"I see your mother is still out there on the floor. It looks like she's found herself a young boy toy. Whew! She looks like she's going to hurt that guy." Calvin and Michelle laughed. "I'm kind of scared of what you're going to do to me when we get to our suite."

"I feel a monster packed behind those tuxedo pants. I'm afraid of what you're going to do to me." She pressed her butt against his groin area.

"You better stop that before Grandma misses out on her dance. And I have a baby to make too? Yeah, you might need to be afraid." He put his mouth closer to her ear and whispered, "And I haven't touched hot, wet pussy in a long, long time."

Michelle could feel an electrical sensation shoot through her entire body. "Damn! You have me wet already. I'm about to say, to hell with Grandma." She laughed, pressing closer into his body.

"Let me go get this dance over with so we can leave," he said before pecking her lips and going for Michelle's grandmother.

"For a minute you almost looked like a couple truly in love."

Michelle's head spun to see the face belonging to the familiar voice. It was Calvin's mother. Michelle knew the woman was going to be a thorn in her side from their first meeting a few months ago.

"Mrs. Edwards. How are you? Are you enjoying yourself?" she tried to say as graciously as possible.

"I probably would be if it wasn't for all this gangster hip-hop music. Who plays this mess at weddings? I've been to tons of weddings and have never heard of such nonsense. It's embarrassing."

Michelle took a deep breath before responding, "I'm sorry you're not enjoying yourself, Mrs. Edwards. I'll be sure to let Calvin know that you had no appreciation for the music *he* selected for our wedding. I told him a band would have probably been much better, but he insisted, and I wanted to be a good wife, and here are the results." Michelle waved her hand at the crowded dance floor.

"Well, I'm sure he was considering what the young people wanted to hear. He's always thinking of everyone else. I swear, I raised that boy to be so selfless."

"Yeah, that must be it," Michelle answered while trying not to laugh.

"Oh my goodness! Who is that old Lucy-Gucy he's on the dance floor with? You can tell she was a loose one back in her day. She ought to be ashamed of herself, shaking herself on my Calvin as if she didn't get one ounce of decent home training." Mrs. Edwards pretended to squint to see her son. "That's your grandmother, isn't it?"

Michelle rolled her eyes and took another deep breath. "Yes, Mrs. Edwards, that is my grandmother you are disrespectfully talking about."

"They say the best way to tell a tree is by its fruit. If that's any indication of the grandchildren I'll have, I don't know. And isn't that your mother over there chasing that poor young boy all over the place?" she asked. "I guess you're the fig nut that didn't fall too far from the tree. Like mother, like daughter."

"You know, Mrs. Edwards, I was really hoping to have a good relationship with you, but you're making it difficult by insulting me and my family. I'm sure Calvin—I mean my husband—would appreciate it if his mother and his wife got along. Don't you think?"

"Michelle, I'll be quite honest with you. I don't like you, my family doesn't like you, and we think Calvy could have done so much better than some desperate woman who talks about love and then exercises poor judgment by running to the altar in less than six months. You have to know my Calvy does not love you. He's only marrying you to get this promotion and he wants children. You're nothing more than an arrangement, and I wish he would have found a woman with better hair for breeding babies. And why would he pick such a small woman when he knows there's a chance his son could come out like a little squirt?"

Michelle wanted to strangle her. She fought back the tears that would let Calvin's mother know her words cut like a knife.

"You know what, lady? You need to get your ass on away from my friend, 'cause I don't like your sneaky-ass son, and I don't like you for breeding the unknown evil."

Both Michelle and Mrs. Edwards turned, surprised by the sharp words from Angie.

"What did you say to me?" Mrs. Edwards said extra loud to signal her two nearby daughters and her other family members in the vicinity.

"You heard me. Heifer!" Angie said with her hands on her hips, after putting the two drinks she carried on the table.

Within seconds, Angie and Michelle were surrounded by Calvin's family. Mrs. Edwards wore a wicked smirk upon her face.

"What's going on, Momma?" one of Calvin's sisters asked, peeling her shoes off in anticipation of a fight.

"This girl just called me a name and said our family was evil," Mrs. Edwards said, pointing to Angie who tried not to let her fear show.

Just as Calvin's five-foot-ten sister towered over a five-foot-five Angie, Calvin and David slipped inside of the growing crowd. "Tiffany! What are you doing?" Calvin yelled.

"This chick is talking smack to Momma," Tiffany answered.

"Well, actually, your mother was over here telling me how much she doesn't like me and how unfit I am to breed her grandchildren, and Angie told her to stop saying all of those mean things to me," Michelle clarified.

"Then that was between you and Momma. This trick needs to mind her damn business," another of Calvin's rowdy sisters said to Michelle.

Calvin pulled both Michelle and Angie from the angry Edwards mob. "This is not happening like this."

As much as Angie hated Calvin, she was grateful for the rescue. She didn't even object when David put his arm around her. Michelle's many friends and family were demanding an explanation. Calvin left Michelle and Angie with them while he went to address his own family's outrageous behavior. After that, he made them leave.

Calvin coming to her rescue and putting her before his family caused Michelle to have a whole other level of respect for her new husband. She only hoped that her best friend would also gain more respect for him after saving her from a massive beatdown.

***

Michelle knew she was in for a treat when Calvin could barely keep his hands off of her as they made their way out of the reception area. After her last good pounding seventeen months ago from Tony, Calvin's ten inches of chocolate was just what she needed, and she could hardly wait. After things were settled down, the newlyweds made their escape to their awaiting honeymoon suite at the hotel, where they would stay until they caught a flight to the Four Seasons Resort Maldives at Landaa Giraavaru the following day.

Angie had warned Michelle about going so far away with a man she knew nothing about, but Michelle figured that little altercation would cause Angie to be more accepting of the man she chose for a husband. Michelle also hoped that her friend might consider giving a handsome David the time of day, despite her lesbian persuasion.

5

David

Thanks for joining me for coffee, Angie. Now that my best bud has gone off of the singles circuit, I'm going to have to find new friends to hang with. Or at the very least, I need to get to know you better since we'll be in each other's presence while we share our mutual friends' company."

"Oh, make no mistake about it—Calvin will never be a friend of mine. I know that's your boy and all, but I don't trust his sneaky ass. And don't get any ideas. This is just coffee. We ain't hooking up and doing the double dating thing."

David tried not to let his facial expression show what was really on his mind: slapping the taste out of Angie's rude mouth. In reality, she did turn him on and he had hoped a cup of coffee might eventually get him to a lunch, and then maybe a dinner with her.

He was, however, happy to hear that Angie was not a fan of Calvin's, as she could help him to get the dirt he needed to pull that partnership rug out from under Calvin's obnoxious feet. After seeing Calvin at his own wedding looking quite cozy with another woman, David figured he needed to gather up all the information he could to play his trump card at just the right time. There was only going to be one person selected for partner, and according to David, it certainly would not be Calvin. David could tolerate any other person getting that spot if it were not him, but Calvin was already unbearable, as Calvin felt he knew everything and would treat life as a game of chess, to include his new marriage.

David hoped a coffee or two might help him learn a little more about the woman Calvin chose for a wife. If he could tap that nice ass on Angie, it would be an added bonus. He picked up on the three times she brushed or pressed up against him after the altercation with Calvin's family at the wedding.

"I have no problem with us just having coffee. Also, I completely respect your feelings about my friend. I can admit that, at times, he can be difficult—"

"Not difficult—sneaky! You can't tell me he doesn't have some kind of game going with this marriage. Who runs off to get married after only knowing each other for like five months, if that? As much as I disliked Tony, at least I knew where he was coming from," Angie said, slamming her fist on the table.

"Who is Tony?"

She hesitated. "Oh, that's just Michelle's ex. He was a trifling son of a bitch. That punk *stayed* in Michelle's pocket. Supposedly he was trying to build up a music studio."

"What happened to him? Did she finally give him the boot?"

"PLEASE! He gave her the damn boot after he got some white chick he was banging on Michelle's dime pregnant. He left Michelle, and now Michelle's acting all hard up for a man and runs off with your boy."

"Was that the woman who made the grand entrance at the wedding?" David asked, already knowing he had seen the woman show up several times in the past while he was hanging out with Calvin. Each time Calvin pretended not to know her. David wanted to bring *that* woman to the forefront of Angie's mind.

"Huh? Oh, no. I don't know who that fake-ass bitch was. I told Michelle she should have whipped her ass, coming in there grandstanding and shit. She told me Mr. Sneaky Ass told her that woman was one of the clients from your PR firm who's supposed to be some big-time international model. I'd like to see the bitch's birth certificate, 'cause you can't tell me her ass wasn't born a man. She was just too damn perfect. Any real woman knows those boobs ain't real. Her waistline looks like she's never eaten a piece of meat, and I know she's had work on those lips and her nose. I was curious to see what her ass looked like, but she had all that extra shit on her dress. I'm sure she's had her ass fixed too.

"The crazy thing is, the second I spotted her I thought she must be one of Calvin's sneaky skeletons. Then I wondered if it was the chick who took Tony from Michelle and caused all of that drama on her television show, but that girl would have had a baby just a few months ago, so that couldn't have been her."

"But didn't you say she appeared to have had surgery?" David asked, still probing.

"That wasn't her! I told you already, Calvin said it was a client."

"You know, now that I think about it, she looks like the woman who would always show up at different places when me and Calvin would be out and one time on a trip to Aruba. I asked if he knew the girl and he said he didn't," David blabbed to heighten Angie's suspicions and form an alliance with her. "Maybe the woman from the wedding was someone different because I did see Calvin in the hallway talking to her. I thought maybe Michelle sent him to confront her for trying to crash the reception."

The wheels were spinning in Angie's head, and David could see he was getting through to her the way he needed.

"I knew his ass had a lot of game. Sneaky bastard! I bet that was his ex-girlfriend from not too long ago. He was probably still sleeping with the bitch and that's why he didn't want to have sex until they were married."

"Well, if that's who he was sleeping with, why hide it? Why wouldn't he want me to know? Why not just marry her instead?" David quizzed.

Angie thought for a second as she sipped on her chai latte. "Maybe because his ghetto family wasn't going to accept him with a white woman."

"Hmmm, that's a thought . . ."

"Or maybe the bitch can't give him the precious kids he wants because 'she' is really a 'he.' That would make more sense."

David laughed at the expression on Angie's face. She looked as if she had just solved some great murder mystery from an Agatha Christie novel.

"What's so funny?" she asked annoyed.

"I'm sorry," David said, trying to stop laughing. "It was just how you said it. It made me think of a good murder mystery book. I know one thing, I got a close enough look at her this time and I think I'll remember those ocean blue eyes if I see her pop up ever again. I've been at the firm just as long as Calvin, and I can't say I remember her as a client. But then again, we don't always see each other's clients. I just don't understand why he didn't just introduce her to all of us—"

"That's what I said! That's exactly what I told Michelle, but she wasn't trying to hear shit. She's always accusing me of being jealous when I try to warn her about these low-life assholes she picks up."

"You two were involved?" David asked, catching Angie off guard and causing her eyes to confirm that they were indeed. "You don't have to be embarrassed about it. You already let me know you're a lesbian. I don't have a problem with it. I think it's kind of sexy." David laughed.

Angie turned all shades of pale. "Please don't say a word. Michelle would die if she knew you knew that. She would never forgive me. Please, you have to promise me," she begged.

"On one condition," he answered.

"I am not sleeping with you. Michelle will just have to get over it," Angie replied, folding her arms with raised brows.

David laughed again. "Wow, as tempting as that sounds, I was only thinking dinner. Have dinner with me. My treat."

"I really can't. It wouldn't be a good idea. I wouldn't want you to get the wrong impression."

"Angie! It's just dinner. You have to eat, I have to eat, so why can't we go have dinner together?"

"I can't. That sounds too much like a date. I'm going to have to say no."

"Boy, won't Michelle be pissed—" David teased.

"You wouldn't."

"I would, so have dinner with me."

"Why? Why do you need me to have dinner with you? Go find a date or something to have dinner with. You don't need me," Angie said half annoyed and half flattered.

"I don't *need* to have dinner with you; I'd like to have dinner with you. My best friend just left me and went off and got married so now I don't have anyone to go to dinner with. I just like your company. You're easy to talk to. I can tell you like to have fun despite that tough-girl act, and you're kind of cute, so I don't mind being seen with you."

Angie coughed from choking on her latte when she was about to laugh. "You've got a nerve. How do you know I want to be seen with you?" she asked, trying not to blush. It had been a long time and she was enjoying the attention.

"Now I know I'm a fine-ass brother, so you should be honored to be in my company," he joked.

"I'll admit you're not too bad on the eyes. If I were into men, I guess you'd be a viable candidate—just to look at, though. Still gotta find out if you're like your shiesty friend or not. They say birds of a feather flock together."

"Well, I guess that means you need to have dinner with me so you can determine if I'm shiesty or not. What better way for you to get to know me? And I'll get to find out if maybe you and your girl might be the shysters."

"Yeah, whatever!" Angie laughed, finally letting her guard down. "And if you act right, I'll even find one of my single, heterosexual friends to hook you up with."

"Don't be trying to set me up with some desperate, baboon-looking friend of yours." David laughed.

"Uh-uh, my friends look good. I got an image to protect too, dammit! My friends have to look a certain way, and I have a certain standard for my women too. Even the guys I hang around gotta be all right looking."

"So what time should I pick you up this evening?"

"This evening? I have plans this evening. Actually, I have a date."

"Ooh, that sounds fun. Can I come along? Hell, I'll pay for both dinners." He laughed.

She looked at him as if he was crazy, before saying, "Nah, I don't think so. This one is already on the fence. The last thing I need is some competition. Check with me tomorrow."

David's ego was slightly bruised because he was hoping to bring Angie back over the fence. "Let's just make it for tomorrow at eight."

Angie thought for a moment. "Fine! May as well get this over with, otherwise you'll be blackmailing me from here to eternity."

David smiled, flashing a perfect set of teeth that dazzled even Angie. "And make sure you wear some high-heeled red pumps with your legs showing."

"What the—oh, hold up!"

David laughed again with his hands held up. "Figured it was worth a shot."

"Black patent leather pumps and denim capris," she teased back.

"Damn! For real?" He looked into her sparkling, flirtatious eyes for a clue. "That'll work for me."

Angie stood up. "Well, I better get back to work. Thanks for the latte."

"Thank you for the company," he said, also standing. "I don't know if it's okay to hug you or not. I've never had a lesbian friend before, so I don't know all the rules."

Angie laughed and extended her hand. "Well, how about you just shake my hand for now."

David took it in his two hands and kissed the back of it, sending a bolt of electricity down Angie's spine.

He watched her walk away before he took out his phone to make notes on the info he got from the conversation. He was determined to find out more about the affair between Angie and Michelle. He also wanted the lowdown on the mysterious woman who continually popped up like a stalker, and who Calvin had consistently denied knowing but told Michelle was a client.

While at the reception, David specifically asked Calvin if that was the woman who kept popping up everywhere. Calvin played as if he couldn't tell because he had never paid her much attention before. After David caught the pair engrossed in an intimate looking conversation, David asked Calvin yet again and Calvin again denied knowing the woman. He said she stopped him to congratulate him and began telling a story about something he wasn't paying attention to. David wasn't buying it. He had also wondered if Calvin was using the woman as some type of spy to help torpedo his path to that partner position.

Little did Calvin know, David had decided to throw his hat in the ring and go after the partner spot. A twenty-nine-year-old African-American woman recently made partner, and that made David feel a bit more confident of getting that next spot at thirty.

David preferred to let Calvin remain full of himself and thinking the spot was as good as his. Meanwhile, David had been quietly putting several lucrative deals together that would help him achieve the honor. He wasn't going to have to bamboozle anyone with a sham of a marriage or bring children into a business arrangement.

David knew he was the quieter type that didn't like to blow a lot of smoke. In their industry, being quiet was typically considered an asset. Their firm employed hungry, loud, cutthroat go-getters. David was none of those things. He was simply a man who wanted to make his single mother proud of his honest, hard work. After reaching his peak with the verbal assaults from his longtime friend and co-worker, he realized that the last thing he wanted to happen was for Calvin to become his boss. At present, the two were on a level playing field. He knew if Calvin became his boss, he'd have to quit. Calvin already behaved as if he was the boss man in the office. The senior partners loved the confidence and commanding presence Calvin projected. As a matter of fact, many were helping to groom him. David's strategy would be like Three-card Monte—while everyone was keeping their eye on Calvin, he would slide in with the top performing accounts and solidify the partnership slot. He knew everyone would have no choice but to respect his strategy, as Calvin wouldn't see it coming. Friendship was great and all, but business was business, and through business, David would make his mother prouder than she could have ever imagined. The only thing in the way was Calvin.

6

Angie

Y ou did WHAT?!" Michelle asked, sitting on the edge of the stool in Angie's kitchen, waiting for the lunch Angie was preparing.

Angie was embarrassed to say the words out loud again. "I slept with David," she sheepishly repeated. "Don't ask me how. I still can't believe it."

Michelle giggled through her shock. "Was it good?"

Angie became flushed. She bought a moment of time by stirring her pot of chili and replacing the lid before answering. "Girl, like you wouldn't believe. His ass had me reevaluating my homosexuality. He ate me so good, he could give women lessons on how to make a woman feel good. Now you know I wasn't quite feeling the dick thing, but I figured, 'what the hell,' and that shit was the bomb-diggity-bomb!"

"Dayum! Like that?"

"Like that!"

Michelle held her hand up for a high-five, but Angie rolled her eyes and waved her away as she pretended to be busy wiping her stove and counter.

"Are you going to see him again?"

"No! Absolutely not! I didn't mean for that to happen. I can't see him anymore. I thought he would be a pretty decent friend to kick it with if your ass was preoccupied with marriage, but now I don't even want to be in the same room with him. That'll be so awkward. Now if the four of us were to go out somewhere together, it would be like a double date. Can't do it!" she answered, taking a seat on the stool next to Michelle's.

"I think you're right. It's probably best you two don't get hooked up. The last thing I need is for you two to have drama and cause drama in my marriage."

Angie looked at Michelle to read her unenthused reaction, which was unexpected. "Well, if anything's going to cause your marriage drama, it's that little-ass dress you're wearing. I can't believe you came out wearing that—that your sneaky-ass husband would let you out with that shit on. Hell, it's turning me on, so I know all the guys out here were getting excited. What gives?"

Michelle looked down at her revealing dress and shrugged. She wasn't too sure why she pulled it from her closet to wear to her friend's home for lunch. "Nothing," she responded dryly.

Angie wasn't convinced. "What's going on? I figured you'd still be getting your world rocked. You just got back from your honeymoon yesterday, so why aren't you at home christening every room in that big house of his? What's the matter, his family came there? What's wrong with you?" Angie finally asked when she saw Michelle's eyes fill with tears.

Michelle took a moment to fight back the tears, but when Angie stood up and hugged her, the tears poured uncontrollably. When she was collected enough, she said, "I married a big dick that doesn't work."

"What? What do you mean by that?"

"He has trouble performing. That night of the reception, he could hardly keep his hands off of me. Once we did make it behind closed doors, I kind of felt he didn't like what he saw once I took the clothes off. Don't get me wrong, he loves the tits, but—I don't know. Maybe I shouldn't be discussing this with you. I have just been bummed the whole two weeks of our honeymoon. Hell, a couple of times he left to take a walk because he was so stressed about the situation. I was happy for the opportunity to satisfy myself. I put this dress on because I needed to feel sexy. Desirable. I don't feel like my husband finds me sexy or desirable."

"So you're saying the whole time you _____
he eat the coochie at least?"

"We had sex, but it was more like a chore_____

"Look, Michelle. I know I'm going to sou___
the scumbag, but I don't think he's the problem.___
same problem with Tony. You'd always talk about ___
you attractive or you thought Tony would fantasize ___
just before touching you. I'm not sure why you are ___
you are fine as hell. Otherwise you couldn't be one of___
bringing a slight smile to Michelle's face. "You are sexy, ___
that to make you feel better. You got more meat on that___
day when we were together, and you know you have filled ___
to know you got a banging body, or else you wouldn't hav___
dressed like that, trying to turn me on and shit," Angie said, ___
in Michelle's space.

"Girl, you better go on somewhere." Michelle playfully swa___

"So what you gonna do? You gonna fuck him for the next ___
your life, always paranoid that he's going to cheat on you and leave___
did with Tony?"

"Paranoid my ass! Tony *did* cheat on me, left me, and married t___
Obviously there must have been something wrong with me."

"Girl, there ain't nothing wrong with you, just your head. You're a ___
nut for thinking like that. Now you're thinking the sneaky ass doesn't find___
attractive. Maybe he just doesn't have any skills. That's probably why he did___
want to sleep with you before the marriage. He knew you would have been lik___
'HELL NO! I am not marrying your ass!' He had to trick you and rush you to
the altar."

Angie embraced her friend for a moment before she said, "The other thing
that I think about is that you're a lesbian trapped in a hetero's body."

"What?" Michelle laughed and pushed Angie away. "How ridiculous! I've
never heard of that nonsense."

bout it. Even before Tony, the jerks you dated couldn't service you
re you able to be satisfied while you and I were together? Were you
n before then? As I recall, when we got together, you told me no
er been able to satisfy you before then. Maybe it's because of that
your grandfather, but still, you've had the same problem with just
ry man."

elle searched her mind for a rebuttal, but could think of none.

ybe part of your problem is that you're so uptight. You don't know
relax. You're on this 'I-gotta-have-a-baby-by-thirty-one' shit and it's
g you. Relax!"

ngie stood behind Michelle and put her hands on her shoulders for a
ge. For a minute, Michelle was very tense, but then she closed her eyes
lowly allowed herself to succumb to Angie's magic fingers. Angie became
e turned on by the minute as she touched Michelle's silky smooth skin.
en she unfastened the hook holding the top part of Michelle's dress up,
re was no protest. Slowly but surely, Angie's hands reached around Michelle
d caressed her bare breasts as she breathed warm air into her ear.

Michelle relaxed completely as Angie slid the small dress past Michelle's
ips and to the floor. She gently touched her pubic hairs as Michelle trembled
with excitement. Her tongue passed her lips to enter Michelle's ear as her
fingers massaged deeper until they found a wet clit. Michelle moaned as Angie
went in deeper with her fingers and her tongue.

Angie made her way in front of Michelle to take her tongue. Michelle was
losing herself in the ecstasy of Angie's touch. Angie sat Michelle back onto the
cold stool and parted her legs, touching her nectar and nibbling on her breasts.
When Angie's fingers were deep inside of Michelle, Michelle held Angie's head
against her bosom for dear life. She gyrated her hips with her thighs spread
apart to allow Angie deeper access. Angie's touch was able to soothe the raging
storm building inside. Angie nibbled her way down Michelle's tight abs until
her tongue found the clit. She gently sucked as her fingers thrust deeper and

deeper inside of Michelle's erupting cave, causing Michelle to release faint screams. Michelle was pressing her pelvis at a rhythm to match the work Angie was putting in.

But then Michelle's cell phone rang, snapping her back to reality. She grabbed her phone from the counter, as she tried to catch her breath. She moved Angie away from her, grabbed her dress from the floor and ran to the bathroom. When she returned from the bathroom crying and dressed, she quickly told Angie that she had to leave, adding that she made a big mistake. She apologized and ran out the door without ever getting to eat the meal Angie prepared for her.

At that moment, Angie knew that she would do whatever necessary to win Michelle back where she belonged. She even thought of seeing David again so she could find out more information about the mysterious woman who kept popping up on Calvin. One way or another, she was going to reclaim her woman, at the same time shaking David from her system.

7

Calvin

Ooh baby, that feels so good. Fuck this pussy!"

The more she talked nasty, the more turned-on Calvin became. It felt like an eternity when it had only been a week. Being intimate with his wife was more unbearable than he could have imagined, but lucky for him, Julissa showed up in Maldives, unbeknownst to Michelle. He was able to sneak away for stolen moments with the one who really was able to satisfy his loins.

For some reason, Calvin would enjoy being affectionate with Michelle, but when it came to slapping skin, he would feel sick to his stomach. He tried to stay focused on impregnating his wife to help him achieve the partnership position. The senior partners let him know that they needed a family man who was able to relate to many of their big-dollar clients with families of their own.

In his perfect world, Julissa could be his wife and they'd have children together. Unfortunately, Julissa wasn't engineered to produce children, but in Calvin's opinion, she was a dream come true and was engineered perfectly for his liking.

"Let me taste that beautiful cock in my mouth."

"Ooh baby! You know you suck it better than any man I've been with."

"I told you I don't want you with anyone else."

"Calvin, don't start. Let's just enjoy this time together. Look, you're making me lose my hard-on.

"Well, I'm not worried about that because I know how to get it back up. I just want you to promise to stay away from any other men. You know I don't like sharing you."

"Well, I don't like sharing either, and now I have to wait for you to steal a moment from that bitch you married. That's not fair to me, Calvin. You know I have my needs too. While that cunt is sucking on your dick, who's supposed to be sucking mine? Who's supposed to be stroking this ass while you're stroking her ass? And you know how I love these titties sucked," Julissa said, cupping her manufactured breasts.

Calvin's face dove into them and begin sucking. After nibbling his way down her flat stomach, he took her natural born eight-inch penis deep into the back of his mouth and sucked it as Julissa fondled his dick, which had just stroked her in the ass. She referred to it as her *pussy*.

Julissa enjoyed living the best of both worlds as a transsexual. She loved the feeling of her dick inside of a man's ass. She enjoyed receiving oral gratification. For her, living life as a gorgeous woman envied by natural-born women was a phenomenal experience. Prior to Calvin, all of her experiences were strictly casual. She met Calvin through one of his clients, who brought him to an exclusive club where Julissa was a regular. Calvin got a kick out of the fact that there was no way a person could tell Julissa was a man without seeing her penis. He took her out many times just to see if people could tell. Instead, Calvin found himself fighting off the many men who would attempt to hit on Julissa. On occasion, a dyke tried to pick up Julissa. Calvin became more territorial with Julissa and, before long, their relationship became sexual. At first, Calvin was not receptive of being on the receiving end, anally speaking. Eventually he opened up and they had been enjoying one another ever since.

Calvin still would not consider himself a gay man because Julissa had the perfect body of a twenty-five-year-old woman—with the added bonus of a dick. As Calvin's feelings grew for Julissa, sleeping with real women became more difficult. He also had no desire to be with any other men or transsexuals. He was in love with Julissa and she with him.

After their lovemaking and their shower together, they sat to talk before he had to make his way back home.

"How long are we going to have to live like this, Calvin? I want to be with you every day. They have places that we could be married. We don't have to tell anyone that I have extra parts. Who's going to try to look?"

"Julissa, stop it! We've already talked about this. You know I had to do what I had to do. It's done now. Hell, you popped up in the Maldives and spent one week out of my two-week honeymoon with me. I'm here with you now. You know how much I need that promotion, and the last thing I need is someone digging up some scandal on me."

"So what's supposed to happen if that cunt gets pregnant? Where will that leave me?" Julissa asked.

"That's the whole point. I'll get my promotion and then I'll really have a good excuse for not being home. My mission will be accomplished, leaving you and I much more time to be together."

Julissa's face lit up. "Really? You promise?" she asked, kissing all over Calvin's face. Calvin sealed his promise with a kiss to Julissa's lips and then another round of lovemaking before he went home to his wife.

8

Michelle

"Sweetheart, do you find me attractive?" Michelle asked, posing in front of a full-length mirror.

"Are you kidding? You're absolutely gorgeous. I get a kick out of just watching you. I even watch you when you're sleeping, and I always try to carve out time in my day to watch your talk show."

Michelle smiled. Calvin's words made her day. "Oh baby, you don't know how much I needed to hear you say that."

"Why would you question something like that? You're the woman I chose for a wife. You're the one I want to wake up to each morning. And I'm going to love watching you as our baby grows inside of you."

"What if I get fat? Are you still going to find me attractive?"

"Michelle, where is all of this coming from? Why are you being so insecure right now?"

Michelle twirled her fingers together. She was nervous, but she knew she could no longer put this conversation with her husband off.

"I sometimes feel that you're not attracted to me sexually."

"As much as we make love? How could you feel like that?

She looked away from him, biting her bottom lip. "That's just it. We hardly make love. Days go by before you try touching me. We've been married two months now. We've made love about fifteen to twenty times total. And even then, most of the time it's quick."

Calvin looked hurt. "I'm so sorry, Michelle. I hadn't realized that I was not satisfying my wife. I don't want to be selfish. If you won't mind showing me what you need to be satisfied, I don't mind learning. I want my wife to be happy. If we need to get some of those toys to help, I'm fine with whatever it will take to please you. Just as long as it's not another man—or Angie, since I see how territorial she behaves with you," Calvin said, searching his wife's face for a reaction.

The smile quickly disappeared from Michelle's face. She wondered just how much her husband knew. She couldn't stop dreaming about that day Angie was on the verge of bringing her to an orgasm. Working together over the past month and a half was getting tough because she needed to shake Angie from her system. What she once shared with Angie had long been over. However, she had no explanation why she felt the need to wear the seductive dress to Angie's for a private lunch. Deep down, she needed Angie's validation. She didn't want to be with Angie intimately anymore, but she wanted to wow her. It went a little further than a wow. It was more of a "wow" for Michelle.

"What would make you say something like that?" she asked.

"Trust me. I see how she looks at you. I am a man. We can see these things. I bet you didn't know that David had a thing for you too."

"David? Your friend David?" she asked, as she went back to the sofa to take a seat next to her husband.

Calvin wore a Cheshire cat smile on his face. "Yep! Confession ... I stole you from David. When you and I first met, I was so preoccupied with business that I hardly noticed how beautiful you were. David asked me about hooking up with you, and then I realized I was sleeping on an opportunity of a lifetime. Seven months later, here we are as husband and wife. That is, if I can keep your friend from knocking me off so she could take you from me." Calvin laughed.

Michelle nervously bit her bottom lip again before answering. "First, you have to understand that Angie is my best friend. We've been besties for almost thirteen years now, so there's bound to be some territorialism in the friendship. I'm sure David probably is just as territorial with his best friend," Michelle said and Calvin laughed, confirming her words. "Besides, I don't think you have a thing to worry about."

"Why is that?"

Michelle looked around the large living room as if there were listening ears. Then she whispered, "David and Angie have been—you know . . ." Michelle gestured with her hands to indicate having sex.

Calvin's mouth dropped open in shock. "No! You're kidding!"

Michelle nodded her head. "Yes. And no kidding."

"When? How? How did I miss that one?" Calvin laughed.

"Please don't say a word. Angie would never forgive me if she knew I told."

"But she's a lesbian. What's up with that? How do you go from being a lesbian one day to heterosexual the next?"

"I didn't say she has given up being with women. I just know she's been seeing David. Keep in mind, she does have a son. I think they got together last week with her son and his daughter and went to Six Flags. She said they had a wonderful time."

"Really! I can't believe David didn't say a word. That sneaky devil."

"Whatever you do, please don't say anything. Let him be the one to bring it up to you."

"Well, how long has it been going on?"

"I think since our wedding. She told me about them when we returned from Maldives."

"Boy, can't you keep a secret," he said, tickling Michelle around the waist causing her to squirm and fall closer into him. "Here all this time I was thinking I had to fight Angie off with a stick to keep her away from my beautiful wife—David, too, for that matter."

Michelle laughed. "Oh, please! I signed up for better or for worse, until death do us apart. You have nothing to worry about."

Calvin gently kissed Michelle. "You mean that?"

"I said it before a packed church, didn't I?"

"Well . . . It's just that you made me a little nervous about the whole sex thing. I want you to believe that I absolutely find you attractive and I get so turned on by just thinking about you while I'm working," Calvin lied. "Nothing means more to me than pleasing my beautiful wife and keeping that pretty smile on her face."

"Oh Calvin, thank you. You have no idea how much that means to me."

"I need for you to always remember that and to believe in me. I know once I get this promotion, it might cause me to be on the road a lot more, but I don't want you to think for a moment that you don't mean the world to me. You are the sun in my universe, and without you, I could never see myself achieving my dreams."

"Wow! The sun in your universe?" She laughed. "That's a high expectation to live up to. You sure you're talking about me?"

"I became sure the minute you said 'I do.' And once we get pregnant, I will feel like the most fulfilled man on this planet."

"Well before you say another word," Michelle nervously turned and looked into Calvin's warm brown eyes, "I just saw my doctor this morning. I'm five weeks. We're going to have a baby."

Calvin was once again shocked.

"Close your mouth before the flies get in," she said, playfully placing her hand over his opened mouth.

"It's just that—Are you serious? I'm going to be a father and you're going to be a mommy? We're going to be parents?"

"Yes, my dear. We are going to be parents. That would explain my twenty trips to the bathroom per day. That may also explain my insatiable sexual desire to be with my husband." The word *insatiable* was a far stretch from the minimal sex life they shared as newlyweds.

"Well, as I said before, I will do all that I can to put and keep a smile on that beautiful face. If you'd like, I can hire a nurse or something to look after you while you're carrying the baby. You know I don't want anything to happen to either of you. Maybe you shouldn't be going up and down the stairs too often."

Michelle laughed. "Calm down, sweetie. I'll be just fine. Nothing's going to happen to me. Between you, Angie, and my overprotective mom and grandma, I'll probably get annoyed from not having a moment's peace for myself."

"Did you tell the others yet?"

"Of course not. How could I tell anyone before I tell my own husband? If you don't mind, I'd like to at least wait until I reach my second trimester before we share our good news."

"Michelle!" Calvin pouted. "How long is that? I was thinking about getting a billboard announcement tomorrow."

Michelle playfully punched his arm. "You're so crazy. That's why I love you so much." She kissed Calvin since that's what he'd always do rather than use the *L* word in return. "The first trimester is the most important time in the baby's development. A lot of women who miscarry do so during this time. I just feel, the less people that know right now, the less stress on me as I protect our child. I already know how your family feels about me, so I can just imagine how relentlessly they'd traumatize me until my uterus was emptied of our baby."

Calvin nodded in agreement. "As embarrassing as that is to admit, you're probably right. What about your friend? Do you plan on telling her?"

"I was thinking that maybe we could have a nice dinner party here and get everyone together all at the same time and make the announcement once I hit twelve weeks."

"That sounds like a good idea, but maybe we should have it at a restaurant or something. Maybe some place where we don't have to worry about world war three again. Also, so we won't have to clean up or anything."

Michelle laughed. "You're probably right."

"I'm your husband. It's my job to be right. Now I have to think about three of us. I darn sure better get things right."

"Well, how about I start off showing you one thing to get right?" she said seductively as she took his hand to rub between her legs. Calvin's hand tensed up. "Just relax, baby. You're going to do just fine."

"I just don't want to mess up again. I'm still embarrassed that I haven't been satisfying my wife."

Michelle pulled Calvin's lips closer to hers as he massaged between her legs, eventually sliding her panties over to touch her wetness. She coaxed his tense fingers inside of her as she kissed him more intensely and massaged his manhood until it was out of his pants and semi-hard.

As she worked his fingers deeper inside her to a place of ecstasy, he asked, "Will this hurt the baby?"

"Not at all. This makes Mommy and baby happy, especially when Daddy kisses the baby."

Calvin looked as if he saw a ghost.

"Calm down, baby. You'll do just fine. I'm going to help you," she said, kissing his lips again to get him to relax.

The more he relaxed, the better his fingers felt inside of her. Her juices were dripping and wetting her panties. Her moans were turning him on and made him explore deeper inside of her, causing her to cry out in joy. After her first orgasm, she stopped him long enough to peel the wet panties off and guide him to his knees in front of her still dripping pussy.

"Take a deep breath and smell it," she instructed him. She massaged herself and then gave her fingers to him to suck on. He sucked her fingers as if he were trying to make them cum. Michelle pulled them from his mouth long enough to replenish them with her juices.

After a few moments, she brought his face to the intended target between her legs. Again he tensed up. She took his fingers and guided them inside of her wetness again as he nibbled on her clit. She removed his wet fingers from her pussy and repositioned them to her asshole as she helped his mouth lower to her wet pussy as she gyrated her pelvis to intensify the wonderful feeling.

Calvin was more turned on than ever, having his fingers inside of Michelle's asshole for the first time. He ate Michelle's pussy as skillfully as he had before he met Julissa, when he only slept with natural-born women.

Michelle didn't know what got into Calvin, but she was happier than ever before. Any thoughts of her ever being with Angie again flew out the window. And when Calvin penetrated her pussy with the hardest dick she'd had in their two months of marriage, she knew no one could ever come in between them. She was caught off guard when he attempted to penetrate her asshole.

"Whoa, baby! I don't know if I'm ready for all of that," she said in between pants and heavy breathing.

"Huh?" he asked. "I thought that's what you wanted?" he asked as his hardness began slipping away.

"I've never had it in the back door. Fingers are one thing; a monster sized dick is another."

He kissed her face and then her lips. "Please, baby. I'll go extra easy. I want to make you feel so good."

"I'm scared. It's going to hurt."

"Not if you'll just relax. You're going to feel so good that you probably wouldn't ever want it any other way. Just relax. Let me be your chocolate god."

Michelle giggled in between kisses, and Calvin again stimulated her clit and took her breath away. "Okay, my chocolate god. Just go easy."

Calvin's dick became harder than during any dick-sucking she had ever given him, just by giving him the green light to go into her back door. He picked his bride up from the floor they were on and carried her upstairs to their bedroom. He searched for some lubricant and went on to give Michelle the best sex she'd had in all her life. In fact, it was so great that both of them called out sick from work that next day to continue to bask in their newfound sexual bliss.

9

David

So where were you yesterday? It's not like you to miss work," David asked, coming into Calvin's office.

"Hey, what can I say? I'm still a newlywed." Calvin chuckled.

Well, there goes Angie's 'Calvin must be gay' theory out the window, David thought and smiled to appease Calvin. "Must have been some day. I don't think I've ever witnessed you this relaxed and happy."

"Man, you just don't know. But what's been going on with you, you sly dog? You know I've been hearing some things about you. Why don't you tell me about this new lady in your life?" Calvin asked, grinning ear to ear.

"New lady? What new lady?" David asked with a look of confusion.

"You and Angie? You weren't going to tell me about that? That's a biggie. You know you're the man when you turn a lesbian back to straight."

"Angie? Angie and I are just friends," David said with a poker face, trying to look surprised by the news. "Nah, she's made it perfectly clear that she is a lesbian and I respect that. Where would you get the notion that we are a couple?"

Calvin looked totally confused. "You didn't hook up with Angie?"

"We had coffee a couple of times. I think we may have had dinner once or twice, but nothing formal."

"Dinner? That's big! How'd that come about?" Calvin quizzed.

David laughed. "What's up with the questions, dude? I was with my daughter at the mall and ran into Angie with her son. They were cordial so I offered a bite to eat since we were standing near the food court at the time."

"The food court? You call eating at the food court, dinner? That doesn't even count."

"My point precisely. That's why I'm a little confused about all this 'hooking up' stuff you're talking about."

"Yo, man, I'm sorry. I'm not sure why Michelle was under the impression that the two of you were now a couple. You know how women can be. They take one small thing and blow it out of proportion." Calvin chuckled just before taking a sip of his coffee.

"So what's up with Julissa Winters?" David asked.

The question caught Calvin off guard, causing him to choke and spill coffee on his crisp white shirt.

"Oh fuck! Oh hell!" Calvin shouted, quickly wiping the coffee as it began to stain his shirt.

"Damn! I'm sorry. I didn't know this Julissa was a sensitive topic," David threw out while he studied Calvin's awkward reaction.

Calvin quickly rose from his desk to close his office door and whispered, "You have it all wrong. Julissa Winters is a potentially big account for me. Handling that account will be great for my chance to make partner. How did you find out about her?" Calvin asked, taking off of his stained shirt to change into a replacement he had in his office closet.

"She approached me yesterday evening in the garage," David lied. "She kind of demanded to know where you were at and wanted to know why you were missing from work—"

Calvin nervously chuckled, cutting David off. "See? I told you—a client. Very demanding, but the account will be great for my portfolio."

"Oh, I see." David laughed. "Perhaps I should have finished my sentence. She said you two were supposed to have a lovely evening out on the town, but instead you were probably laid up with that—quote, unquote—bitch of yours that you only married to get the partnership."

Calvin was rendered speechless. He looked ashen, as if all the warmth had left his chocolate complexion. Beads of sweat had formed over his brow.

David waved his hand in dismissal. "Man, you ain't gotta worry. Your secret's safe with me. You know I'm not trying to throw any salt up in your game."

"I . . . I . . . She—We . . ." Calvin stuttered.

"Don't even sweat it, dude," David said as he made mental notes while studying Calvin.

Calvin finally got his bearings together to form yet another lie. "That woman is crazy. She's just a client. That's it! She's just very demanding of my time."

"And you don't have the account yet?" David asked suspiciously.

"I'm very close. She was probably just angry because I was supposed to take her to the jazz bistro up the street—Oh yeah, and I totally forgot while being with my wife. I even mentioned the meeting to my wife. My wife tried to push me to go to my meeting, but I could hardly tear myself away from her. That's why I'm glad to have my wife," Calvin repeated like a broken record.

"Okay! I got it! You have a wife. That was like ten 'my wife's' in three sentences. I already told you, your secret is safe with me." David laughed. "It's not that serious."

"I'm not having any affairs. I am a newlywed and I'm about to be a father—" Calvin covered his mouth.

"You're going to be a father? Oh man! This is big," David said, extending his hand to shake Calvin's non-extended hand. "No wonder you missed work."

"Aw crap! Please, please don't say a word. Michelle made me promise that we were going to tell everyone in one big announcement. She would strangle me if she found out I slipped this one up."

David pretended to lock his lips. "Not a word from me. I can tell you right now, that it's not going to sit well with your wife's best friend. She's not exactly your biggest fan. She didn't think your marriage would last a whole six months. To be quite honest, after that whole Julissa fiasco yesterday, I started to wonder myself." David's eyes locked onto Calvin's diverting eyes.

Calvin nervously chuckled again. "Well, yeah, I told you, you were mistaken about that. As for that lesbo-bitch, who cares what she thinks? She's probably mad because she wants my wife and my wife ain't thinking about her dyke ass."

"Who knows, maybe the two of them were an item at one time. Has that ever crossed your mind? That would explain the possessiveness," David asked, still probing.

Calvin's jaw tightened. "Okay, I know it's time for you to leave my office. You have just officially grossed me out for the day. The thought of my wife sucking on tits or with her face buried between some bitch's legs—ugh! That's nasty. Get out!"

David laughed. "Hey, the thought turns me on—of two women together, that is. Now that's a fantasy." He continued laughing as he left to jot down some notes about the encounter with his friend-slash corporate nemesis. After entering his notes in his phone, he picked up the phone on his desk.

"Hey, beautiful! You think you could meet me for lunch? Same spot at one."

10

Calvin

Calvin stormed into Julissa's condo filled with rage thirty minutes after his impromptu meeting with David. He tried to suppress the level of anger brewing by the minute inside of him. He poured himself a glass of scotch from the expensive crystal decanter, but his anger caused him to throw it against the white wall, smashing the precious glass into hundreds of pieces. He took a swallow from his glass before also throwing that at the large oval mirror that sat above the fireplace.

"You bitch! You bitch! You stupid fucking bitch!" he yelled out loud.

Calvin paced back and forth throughout the spacious two-bedroom Buckhead condo as he waited for Julissa to arrive. He was waiting to snatch her as quickly as he heard the keys in the door.

"What the—" was all she managed to say before Calvin grabbed her arm and flung her to the cold marble floor in the foyer like a rag doll. Julissa tried to let out a scream, but Calvin repeatedly shook her and even choked her. He snatched her up from the floor, dragging her by her arm to the plush espresso-colored sofa in the living room. He threw her on the sofa as he caught his breath.

"What the fuck is the matter with you?! You're trying to make me lose everything?" he yelled.

Julissa was still shielding her face, her dress was hiked up to her waist, and she was wearing only one shoe at that point. She managed to ask through her sob, "What are you talking about? Why are you doing this to me?" She then looked around from where she lay on the sofa. "What have you done to my home?"

"Your home! I paid for this shit! This is my damn home that I got for us to be together in, and this is how you treat me? You're so fucking dumb. How could you be so damn stupid? Don't you know if people find out about us, I could lose everything? And then you want to act like a fucking lunatic just because you don't hear from me for one fucking day? I have a wife now. It's going to be like that at times. Grow the fuck up! You know what I'm trying to accomplish and you know what's at stake. If I lose everything because you want to act stupid . . ." Calvin held up both of his hands with a deranged look of desperation on his face. "Julissa, I swear to you, if you push me too far, I don't know what I'll do to you."

"What—" Calvin back handed Julissa in the mouth before she could finish her question.

"Just shut the fuck up! The less you say to me right now, the better."

Calvin lifted her by the arm, turned her around, and pushed her back on the sofa again as he reached inside of his pants to pull out his erect dick. Julissa's submissiveness was turning him on. He wanted to get a little before he headed back to the office for his 2 p.m. meeting. He was too wound up to blow the new big client he was trying to acquire for his portfolio and to solidify his run at partner. He ripped the lace panties from Julissa, releasing her limp cock, and forcefully took what he wanted before leaving her distraught.

11

Angie

Well, did you get anything?" Angie asked when David arrived at the restaurant and slid into the booth.

"Like you wouldn't believe, and then some."

"Spill it! Don't keep me waiting."

"Oh, he played right into it. Whoever this Julissa is, the mention of her certainly rattled him big time. He looked as if he saw a ghost," David shared.

"Damn! What did you tell him?" Angie asked, on the edge of her seat.

David took a couple of Angie's French fries and she slapped his hand.

"Now you know better than to mess with my McDonald's fries," she playfully scolded.

He gave her a look of disbelief. "Now you knew I was coming. You should have gotten the extra large. These are my favorites too." He laughed as he crammed the stolen fries into his mouth. "I'll be back. Let me go order some."

He was about to walk away.

"All right! All right! Hold on. Take mine. I need to hear what happened." Angie pushed her tray toward David and he crawled in the booth next to her, grabbed her hand, and kissed it. She snatched her hand and rolled her eyes laughing. "Just spill it!" she commanded.

"I should receive an Academy Award for my performance this morning. He stormed out of the office just as quick as I told him that some woman named Julissa Winters came by causing a scene, demanding to know his whereabouts. I said the lady said that he was supposed to take her to the jazz bistro last night. Well, actually, I just said out on the town and he volunteered the jazz bistro."

"Why'd you say that?" Angie asked. "He would have automatically known it was a lie if he knew he had no plans with the woman or even if he was with her."

"Please! I struck gold with that one." David laughed. "Your boy started offering up all kinds of info, talking about she's a demanding woman and he's just been working on getting the contract from her to help get his spot as a partner. Of course, no senior partner at the firm has ever heard of any Julissa Winters."

"Perhaps they're playing coy with you because of some loyalty to Calvin," Angie offered.

"Nope! She's nonexistent to the company. I heard from my secretary, who heard from the gossip in the secretary's crew, that there was a nutcase a couple of years ago who was trying to make a name for herself in the modeling industry. Apparently she would try to crash celebrity functions to gain publicity for her career."

"Then maybe this whole thing is, in fact, innocent then. That would explain the chick crashing the wedding the way she did."

David looked at Angie as though she were stupid. "Please tell me you don't believe that."

"I'm just saying." Angie hunched her shoulders and laughed.

"You know, as much as I enjoy the sex with you, we both have missions we're trying to accomplish. I'm trying to get that 'token nigger' partnership slot with the firm."

Angie burst out laughing. "Token nigger? Is that how you view it? And you actually have the nerve to be fighting for that?"

"You damn right. They have a bunch of brothers, doing whatever we can to sabotage the other just to get that one slot. How are they going to flat out say 'this position will be for a black male'? How about they should be saying the most qualified will get the slot, despite race, sex, color or what have you. Hell, they even made certain to bring in a Hindu gay woman just to be politically correct. It's a bunch of bullshit, you know."

"So why stay there and complain if you know they are like that? How about start your own PR firm? I think your cute, charming ass has what it takes to be successful. Hell, you charmed the thong off my lesbian ass." Angie laughed. "I think you should tell all of them to kiss your ass and go do your own thing."

David lifted Angie's hand again and kissed it. "You are wonderful. You're the type of woman a man needs in his corner. Still, I could not sit back and let Calvin get that slot in good conscience. Do you know his arrogant ass sometimes has the nerve to make racist comments? He talks about how black people are like backwards-thinking monkeys that will never amount to shit because of their buffoon behavior. When I remind him that he is black, he believes God made him the exception to the rest. He feels he is the only one qualified to excel within the company. He feels black women only get their positions because white men love them some dark berry juice and for no other reason. I'm trying to figure out how he managed to fool Michelle, because the way he talks, it's like he hates women. Especially black women. I just feel sorry for that baby. The thought of having his ass for a father makes me cringe."

Angie looked at David side-eyed before slamming her hand on the table. "Hold up! Stop the freakin' press! What did you just say?"

David looked confused as he tried to think of what he could have said to set Angie off. "What? He hates black women?"

"What *baby*?" she asked.

David covered his face with both of his hands when he realized the slip-up. "Oh shit!"

"David! You knew about a baby and wasn't going to tell me about it?"

"I swear I wanted to tell you the minute I found out this morning. Calvin slipped up and told me and made me swear to secrecy. I was worried about telling you and you blasting Michelle for not telling you, if she hadn't already."

"Here I have been, back-stabbing my best friend to be in cahoots with you, and then you thought I'd go and tell?"

"Well, perhaps I should tell you how my initial meeting with Calvin went this morning. It began with him questioning me about 'our' relationship. Somehow he has learned that you and I have been deeply involved and intermingling families. He made it as if we were about to move in with one another. Where in the Sam Hill did he get that from? Hmmm? I think he said his wife—your best friend and the one you're trying to win back into your bedroom."

Angie had a nervous smile on her face as she put one of her long manicured nails between her teeth. "Damn! That bitch has a big mouth. Where's the loyalty? Geesh!"

David laughed. "So did you tell her I rocked your world or what?"

"Please! I told her you were all right. Figured she might feel a twinge of jealousy and she'd start worrying about losing all of this."

"Really good 'all of this' if I may say so myself. Uhm . . . David Junior is getting excited."

"Whatever! I already told you I'm nipping that shit."

"You said that like ten times now. How am I supposed to take you serious? You wanna have dinner tonight?"

"Your place or mine?" Angie asked without hesitation.

"I'm good with either. So are we still supposed to be a secret or what? You can't say you don't want Michelle and Calvin to find out one minute, but the next minute you're the one blabbing."

"I really didn't want them to know but, damn, shit was good and I needed to tell someone. I couldn't tell anyone else because then I'd lose my lesbian title. I'd be called 'confused.'"

David's ego was grinning ear to ear. "I think having a warm-blooded dick up inside of you like two or three times a week trumped your lesbian card a long time ago. When was the last time you've been with a woman?"

David stared as she tried to look away.

"That's a very personal question. Hell, we're only supposed to be 'Michelle and Calvin espionage' partners . . . with benefits." She laughed.

"Well, you're not being a very good spy partner, slipping up telling that we have been seeing each other. You're supposed to hate me and talk about me in a bad way to get her talking about Calvin's thoughts and plans about me. You're not supposed to be talking about me in a Michael Jackson 'Bad' kind of way."

"You're a nut!" Angie said, hitting his arm as they laughed at David's joke.

"I'm just saying. You're going to have to stick with the plan, girl. Who knows? Maybe if I'm lucky, I'll get the job and the girl," David said flirtatiously.

"David Mosely, are you catching feelings here?"

"I was in love with you from the moment you pushed your fries in my direction. Who wouldn't love a woman who gives up her McDonald's fries? Giving up pussy is one thing—even tight lesbian pussy. But the French fries? That's big."

"Boy, you're stupid!" Angie said, cracking up.

David stood up before bending down to peck Angie's lips. "Call me later, beautiful. I'm going to cook dinner for you tonight."

"Hmm, sounds like a plan," she responded, still cherishing the warmth left lingering from his full lips against hers.

Angie sat kicking herself. The game plan was going all wrong. The original plan was to play David long enough to get the necessary information to destroy Calvin and get him out of Michelle's life. After having given up her order of French fries to him, she too began to wonder just how deeply her feelings had gotten caught up.

The reality was that it had been almost a month since she was with another woman or anything else. Even her vibrating rabbit hadn't been getting any attention since David had been handling business. She was also beginning to lose sight of the objective of the plan, which was to get Michelle back as her lover.

Angie thought Michelle's pregnancy may throw a wrench in the plan—

that is, if she didn't lose the baby. Michelle didn't even have the decency to tell her closest friend about the baby, and Angie hated that Michelle had to blab to Calvin about her being with David.

No loyalty!

12

Michelle

Angie, I am so afraid. That's twice in the past eight days that my windows have been busted out."

"What are the police saying?"

"Nothing! They asked me to make a list of all the people who hate me."

"Did you tell them you host a relationship talk show? You'd have a whole laundry list of haters," Angie volunteered. "Do you think it could be Tony's baby momma again? That little nut seems to come out of the woodwork with her madness."

"Oh my goodness! I don't know what I would do if it were her. Damn, she's married to Tony and has a child with the cheating bastard. Not only that, I'm married now. Why wouldn't she just leave me alone?"

"Well, what about that other nut that showed up to your wedding like a bitch with an ax to grind?" Angie asked. "I told you there was something suspect about her ass the moment I spotted her."

"You know, it's funny that you mention her, because I think I saw her at Lenox Square yesterday. I couldn't be certain. I remember she had pretty blue eyes and healthy brunette hair. Plus, she was tall and gorgeous."

"Gorgeous my ass! '*Georgeous*' if anything. That bitch looked like a tranny. I bet you she is packing between the legs." Angie laughed.

"Eew! That's nasty. Don't even say stuff like that. I'm getting sick to my stomach just thinking about it."

"You've been getting sick to your stomach about everything lately. You have something you need to tell me?"

Michelle chuckled nervously. "I don't think so."

"Uhmm-hmmm. If you say so."

"But getting back to my situation with the window, what am I going to do, Angie? This is getting scary. I really don't need this stress right now of all times."

"Why? What's so important about right now?" Angie continued probing, wondering when Michelle would confess.

"I mean I have a new marriage and I don't need for my husband to see me come undone," Michelle lied.

"Please! What do you really know about him? For all you know, he could be breaking your windows to creep you out. Maybe one of his bitches on the side is coming after you. That's usually the most logical thing. I'm sure even the police asked you that."

Michelle paused as she thought back to the police suggesting exactly that. "You know, Angie, I'm getting kind of weary of all the cheap shots you take at my husband. We are married until death does us part. He's not going anywhere. I'm not going anywhere, so back off and show some respect."

Michelle could hear Angie choking and getting her bearings together through the telephone. "How about you call your damn *husband*, wherever he may be at almost midnight, and dump on him about how scary your ass is. What the fuck are you bothering me with it for? And I just want you to know, since the sneaky bastard came into your life, you have changed. And trust, that is no compliment. I'll see you at the studio tomorrow. Good night!"

"Angie, wait a minute. This is getting out of—" Michelle started before she heard a dead silence. "Angie? Angie?"

There was no response.

"Bitch!" Michelle yelled as she put the phone down.

Outside of the car window incidents and Calvin's job, things had been going blissfully well for Michelle and Calvin for the past three weeks since finding out about the baby. Calvin had been extra attentive and extra affectionate, and they'd been having hot, steamy sex . . . except for the past five sexless days. They shared a lot of laughter. Michelle wasn't the happiest with the anal sex, but she loved that they were having plenty of sex.

Earlier that morning she became snappy as her fear began to set in. When she left her office, both front windows of her Pathfinder had been broken out. Nothing was taken. The first act of vandalism was more horrific. The back window of her Beamer was busted and a bloody rabbit was thrown into the back seat. She immediately thought someone was paying her back because of a recent ad for her talk show, which pictured her wearing a white mink coat. The ad read, "When it's cold outside, come inside with Michelle, where it's hot." As much was spent on the ad, the ad was immediately pulled. Still, someone felt the need to break out her windows as quickly as she replaced the first one.

It was almost midnight, and Calvin had yet to call and say he'd be home late. Michelle accepted the fact that taking her frustrations out on her husband that morning may have been the reason for his silent treatment. She even told him, "Check your bitches!" He looked stunned as well as genuinely hurt. He kissed her goodbye and left in silence. Her three calls to him went unanswered. His secretary informed her that he had a last-minute meeting with some clients that evening, but Calvin didn't bother to tell her.

At 1:17 that morning the doorbell rang. It was as if Michelle had just dozed off. She looked at the other side of the empty bed and realized that Calvin still hadn't made it home. Fear gripped her as she heard the ringing become more persistent. She didn't know if the police were coming to deliver some bad news or if it was an intruder. She eliminated the intruder theory because they were persistently ringing the bell.

After slipping on a robe over her gown, she crept through the dark room to see out of the window for any sign of a police car. Instead, she saw David's black SL6. She turned on some lights and made her way downstairs to the door.

"David, what on earth are you doing here this time of night?"

David looked beyond disgusted. "Your husband is passed out in my car. He had way too much to drink and lost his keys."

"Are you serious?"

David chuckled through his anger. "The grimy bastard was meeting with one of my clients behind my back, got a little too intoxicated, and who did they have the nerve to call? Me! Fucking me, who knew nothing about the meeting. David to the fucking rescue. Doesn't matter that I have a knife in my back and one in the gut. That's what friends are for."

"Oh David," Michelle said when uncovering her mouth. "I am so sorry about that. I can't imagine what that could be all about since Calvin and I never discuss his business. We had a bit of a spat this morning because I was getting scared about the vandalism to my cars. Please don't be angry with him. It was my fault for pushing him too far."

David looked at Michelle as if she was either crazy or unable to comprehend the brevity of what Calvin had attempted to do by meeting with David's client behind his back. "Michelle, your husband—my best friend—was attempting to steal my clients until he became too inebriated to finish the deal and they called me. Never mind! I don't know why I'm even telling you this. You two were probably in on it together," he snapped, flailing his arms up in the air. "Let me get your husband out of my car so I can get back home."

Michelle had tears in her eyes. She was hurt to know what her husband would do to his best friend for the sake of that partnership position.

David helped Calvin as far as the bench in the foyer and then turned to Michelle. "You sure know how to pick 'em, Miss Relationship Expert," he said before storming out.

Michelle went back to bed and cried herself to sleep, leaving Calvin on the cold foyer floor where he fell right after David helped him to the bench.

When Michelle woke at six-thirty, Calvin still hadn't made it to bed. She went downstairs to find him in the exact same spot, balled up, looking as if he was cold. She wondered if he was dead, but when she was about to feel for a pulse, he moved and groaned.

"Calvin! Calvin, get up! Do you hear me? Get up!"

Calvin slowly began to rise up from the floor, but he vomited as quickly as he made it to his hands and knees. The sight nauseated Michelle, and she bolted to the bathroom before her morning sickness began kicking in.

Calvin stumbled, holding his head to the half bath, where Michelle was throwing up. "I think someone drugged me."

Michelle lifted her head from the toilet, half not giving a damn about his problems, as hers seemed more immediate. Abortion came to mind when she had to endure such violent morning sickness, but each time she reminded herself that it was only temporary.

"Did you hear me?" he asked when she failed to acknowledge his earth-shattering concern.

She just nodded her head as her guts unleashed another round of fluids into the toilet.

"Ugh!" he said, turning away. He stumbled his way up the stairs and fell onto the bed.

When she was able to get herself together and make it back up the stairs, Michelle asked, "Aren't you going to clean up your mess in the foyer?"

"The housekeepers will be here soon. Let them take care of it," he answered, still holding his head while lying on his back.

"Ugh! That's disgusting. No one wants to clean up someone else's puke."

"Michelle, please! That's what the hell they get paid for. If I have to clean it, then I don't need to pay them. I'm more concerned about how and who drugged me. I don't even know how I got home or anything. The last thing I remember is that I was having dinner with some potential clients. I don't remember anything else. I don't see my briefcase, my keys, my phone—nothing. Where is my damn car? How did I get here?"

Michelle was annoyed by his comment about the housekeepers, but she was also worried about someone actually drugging her husband. "David brought you home last night. He was quite angry with you. He said something about you stealing his clients and that you ended up getting very drunk before you finished your deal. Someone called him to come and get you. He said you lost your keys. He didn't mention anything else."

"So David brought me home and left me lying on the foyer floor rather than to help me upstairs to bed? How fucked up is that? He's supposed to be my boy and that's how he does me?"

Michelle looked shocked by Calvin's arrogance. "How he did you? You were trying to steal his clients and you expect him to be loyal to you? Be glad he brought you home. He could have left you along the side of any dark Georgia road."

"Are you siding with him, Michelle?" Calvin arrogantly asked, as if that was the most illogical thing he had ever heard. "What, are you two all buddy-buddy now? This is business. David knows that. You need to know that. That's how this business goes. I have a better chance at this partnership than David and he knows it. It would only make sense for him to roll his clients under me, which will be much more beneficial to him in the long run. Michelle, David is my best friend. He was the best man at our wedding. Why in the world would I ever do anything to hurt him? Half the time he doesn't know what's best for him. I am way more talented and strategic than he is, but he can go so much further just riding on my coattails. Otherwise, he is not going far." Calvin patted the bed beside him. "Come sit. Honey, don't let David get inside your head. The thing I admire most about you is your intelligence and your strong mind. Think about our baby. This little one growing inside of you," he said, rubbing Michelle's tiny bulging belly. "To say you don't want me to do what's best in business is like saying you don't want the best for our children. I know you like this house. Wouldn't you like to afford several vacation homes for our family and private schools for our kids?"

Michelle softened up her demeanor and smiled. "I guess you're right."

"And you need to watch what you tell your friend, Angie, as well. I'm not sure why she's telling you she's involved with David and he's saying they are not involved. One of them is lying. I think it's your gay friend. David's not smart enough to snag a heterosexual woman, let alone a lesbian. And if he was, he certainly wouldn't know how to keep it to himself. How do you think I got a list of his clients? Any of the other guys trying to make partner could have gotten the information just as easily. They would have used that information to knock both David and me out of the running for the position."

"It just feels so strange betraying my best friend," Michelle said sadly.

"I can guarantee that she has nothing nice to say about me, our marriage, or our baby when she finds out."

Michelle's eyes confirmed what he was saying.

"Baby, it's you and me against the world. I need you in my corner to get this partnership so we can build an empire together. I need for you to help me get more clients in my portfolio. Maybe you could use some of your connections and send them in my direction. Together, we'd be unstoppable. We'd be the envy of the world. Anything your friend is doing for you, I can do ten times bigger. I could make you the next Oprah if that's what you want. Stay with me and dream big."

"If I cut Angie out, where would that leave her?" Michelle sheepishly asked. "I don't want to hurt her. She's all I have. I don't have any other real friends."

"First, you need to get out of your head that she's your friend. She's only doing what she's doing for you to help herself. She doesn't give a damn about you. You are her meal ticket and nothing more. All she probably thinks about is how to get her face between your legs. She'd probably give you the boot the minute she did. The bitch!" Calvin held his head. "Ow! My head hurts. She—both of them makes my head hurt. I don't even want to talk about them anymore. I need to get to the bottom of who drugged me and took my phone and briefcase."

"Maybe your stuff is at the restaurant. Why don't you call or go by there?"

"Yeah, maybe I'll do that. Changing the subject, what have you heard about your car window?"

"I haven't heard anything. I am so scared. And now with what happened to you . . . I don't know. I'm just worried."

"Do you think you need a bodyguard for when I'm not around?"

Michelle gave it some thought before shaking her head. "Nah. It's not like anyone has tried to do anything to me personally. My car could probably use a bodyguard, though." She chuckled. "And while we're on the subject, I need to apologize to you for my temperamental behavior yesterday morning. It hurt me all day knowing you were upset with me."

"It's no problem, but please keep in mind I need a peaceful household to live in. That's what keeps me on top of my game. I understand your being frustrated and all, but save your wrath for the ones who hurt you, not the only one in your corner," Calvin responded with no sympathy.

Michelle was apologetic, but still she would have appreciated a bit more sensitivity in his words. Instead of responding, she just smiled. Although she was on the snappy side the day before, she continually would apologize in between snaps and explain her frustration about being afraid.

"Well, I better get ready to head to the office," Calvin said, standing up.

"What about your car? Do you need me to take you to your car or the restaurant?"

"Nah, you can just drop me at the office. I need to show my face first. I'll grab a cab later to go pick up my Porsche. I did want to drive the Maserati today, but that'll mean I have to leave the Porsche too long. And you know that won't be happening."

Michelle listened to him with a smile. She hated his seven unnecessary cars that he would often talk her to death about. When her windows were broken on her Beamer first and then the Pathfinder, he had her rent a car while the shop worked on the repairs rather than let her drive one of his status cars.

When he finished going on and on and on about his precious cars, Michelle asked, "Honey, do you think we might have a little time this morning to . . . you know?" She was horny despite everything and somehow five days had slipped by since he made love to her.

"Oh baby, I'm so sorry. I really have to get out of here. I'm already late and I have to find my phone, wallet, briefcase, and keys. I don't know if I have to report the cards lost or what. I wouldn't be any good to you right now while my mind is distracted. Maybe we could plan a nice romantic weekend up in the mountains."

"Tomorrow is Friday. That's not enough time to put something together," she said with disappointment.

"This is Calvin you're talking about. I make things happen, and don't you forget that," he said before kissing her forehead and heading for the shower without his horny wife.

13

David

Y ou know, for as long as I was hung up on that damn girl, she pissed me off today trying to nonchalantly rub her tits up against my back all fucking day," Angie said to a hysterically laughing David. "First she wants to talk shit to me about her *husband,* and then she wants her tits touching on me every five minutes. No bra, of course. Any other day, that shit would have excited me. Not this fucking day."

"Her boobies should be getting bigger since she's pregnant now, shouldn't they?" David asked.

"I haven't noticed a difference. I see her face and ass are filling out. She looks fuller in the face. So many people have already asked if she is expecting and she'll laugh it off with a 'Why would you ask me something like that?' Every five minutes she's running to the bathroom or supposedly ate something that didn't agree with her. Everyone is just supposed to be so stupid and not know any better. I'm just pissed that's she's trying to keep it from me and we're supposed to be best friends, or so I thought. The silly rabbit!"

David laughed harder as he looked at the onlookers in the restaurant giving him a look of chastisement. He simply shook his head at them and rolled his eyes. "I'm still cracking up about that rabbit incident. What made you think of the dead rabbit thing? That was ingenious. Even Mister Loverboy was shaken up by that one."

Angie couldn't help but laugh. She tried to cover her mouth as she too saw the pointed stares. "The rabbit test used to be the way they determined whether or not a woman was pregnant. If the rabbit died, the woman was pregnant, so I used a dead rabbit since I know the bitch is pregnant and wants to deny shit to me. I figured she would think someone was letting on they knew she was pregnant. Didn't think she'd pull the whole ad campaign because of the mink coat. I just wish you would have thrown the rabbit in when you hit the Pathfinder. She would have really wondered what the rabbit symbolized."

"I swear I tried. I couldn't bring myself to touch that dead rabbit. I'll admit, you have more balls than me—no pun intended."

"That's okay. I just love the way you've been handling Calvin. Talk about brilliant. And now that you have the contents of his life in that briefcase, the possibilities are endless."

"I noticed in the call log that he talks to a JW at least three times a day."

"JW being Julissa Winters," Angie confirmed.

"Yep! She calls his phone all through the night. I can't imagine a client or potential client calling me like that. I noticed one text message between them where he wrote, 'Keep it hot. On the way.' There were tons from JW wanting to know where he was at, and I saw that the last message he sent JW was 'Meeting at the mountain house this weekend.' Ironically, you tell me that Michelle tells you Calvin is taking her on a spontaneous romantic getaway to the mountains tomorrow, yet he had this trip planned already. You think Michelle knows JW will be there too?"

Angie rolled her eyes. "Hell no! Maybe we need to go to the mountains this weekend to see what that's all about. I'm curious to see how he pulls this one off. Sounds like it's going to be hot up there. But did you say 'mountain house?' Does he have a house in the mountains as well? How much real estate does his ass have?"

"He has a property up in Tennessee. It's nice. We went up there a few years ago right after he purchased it. There are two really beautiful houses on the land, and he rents them out for vacation rentals. Dude has plenty of real estate. He had a condo in Buckhead before he bought that house he's in now. I never asked him about that. He has a beachfront property on Kiawah Island and he had a rental property with five or six families. He likes to roll his dollars into real estate and his cars. I'm a Dow Jones man myself."

"A well 'endowed' Jones man if I must say so myself," Angie said, raising her eyebrows with a smile.

"Girl, you got me blushing," David said, laughing.

"Hey, if the shoe fits—and I mean a big damn shoe, at that—wear it proudly."

"You're about to make me take you right here in this restaurant. I'll clear off the table, lay you up there, and tear that ass up." He looked into her eyes as if he wanted her to dare him. She didn't. "I thought so," he said when her eyes looked away.

"But anyhow, getting back to business. Is there anywhere up near the house in the mountain that we could go and spy from?"

"Yes and no. There is a funky-looking inn not too far away, but not close enough to see what's really going on. There is a guest house on the property, but I'm thinking that's where he may stash JW. Choice number three is to camp out in the woods like a police stakeout."

Angie looked at David as if he were crazy. "Somehow I think you're serious."

"I am."

"So while they're all snuggled up in front of a romantic fireplace, you want us to be outside freezing, hoping to see something? Is that what you expect?" Angie asked, pretending to be mad.

"We could keep each other warm," David answered, hunching his shoulders.

"And what about all of the wild animals out there?"

"Shit, after the way you massacred that rabbit, those wild animals don't stand a chance with you."

They both laughed so loud, nearby guests at the five-star restaurant turned to look. The *maître d'* approached the table. "Bonjour Monsieur, Madame! Is everything okay?" he asked more scolding than concerned.

"Oui, oui. I apologize for the outburst. It won't happen again," David tried to assure.

The maître d' looked unsatisfied by David's apology but continued to stand there.

In French, David said with a smile, "If you don't mind, I'd like to continue dinner with my lovely date and can do without your chastisement as if we are small children. Please go unless you are called."

"As you wish, Monsieur," the insulted maître d' replied before turning to walk away.

"What did you say to him? He looked pissed. I don't even wanna order dessert now. They might piss in it."

"I told him I am trying to get my mack on with this fine-ass honey and he's messing up my game," David replied before laughing. "And what do you mean dessert? Don't think I haven't tallied up the cost of your meal. That's the equivalent of 'I'm getting some pussy tonight'."

Angie burst out laughing again. Again heads turned to look at them, along with the maître d'.

"Come on, let's bounce. I'm still hungry anyway. We can stop off for an extra large McDonald's fries and a Dairy Queen Banana Split for dessert," David said, standing up and peeling four hundred-dollar bills from his wallet and throwing them on the table.

"You want me to leave the tip?" Angie asked, impressed by his generosity. "I think I have five dollars in my pocketbook," she joked.

He took her hand in both of his hands and kissed it.

"Come on, let's sneak out before they realize we didn't leave a tip," he joked back, since he knew the check wasn't more than $300.

The maître d' looked as if he was ready to stop them from leaving without paying their bill, but the server was at the table to collect the money. He gave the maître d' a nod.

"Have a pleasant evening and do come again," the maître d' politely spoke.

"I don't think I'll make that mistake again," David answered as he escorted Angie out of the restaurant. "I'm going home to get some punani. That's a real meal." He smiled and winked.

14

Calvin

O h Calvin! This place is beautiful. I can't believe you found it on such short notice," Michelle said as she looked around the log-style house in the mountains of Tennessee. Surrounding the open floor plan kitchen, living room, and dining area were three equally large dual-leveled master suites, two smaller bedrooms, an office, and one and a half bathrooms.

She walked to the window. "This place could comfortably sleep fourteen people without them getting in each other's way. Looking at it from the outside, I would have never thought it was this spectacular. I wish I could see inside the house next door. It's probably just as fabulous."

"Gee, how about focus on your husband rather than what's outdoors?" Calvin laughed before kissing his wife.

"Hmm, sounds like a great plan." She turned around and wrapped her arms around his neck. "I'm going to go get cleaned up and begin fixing dinner."

"Okay, great! I'm going to head down the hill to the store before they close. I want to pick up a few emergency supplies to keep up in here. I should have stopped before we came all the way up."

"Emergency? What type of emergency?"

"Don't start to panic. The power could go out. We could use some extra water, and I might have to pick up some extra logs for the fireplace. I'm trying to romance this beautiful woman that happens to be carrying my child," he told her as he ran his hands up and down her shoulders to reassure her.

Her eyes smiled, letting him know she was okay. "Just hurry back. As beautiful as this place is, it's still scary being here all by myself, especially with all the stuff happening to us lately."

"Sweetie, you'll be fine. I won't be gone more than an hour. It's about a twenty-minute drive to town."

"Wow, twenty minutes to civilization." Michelle closed her eyes and took a deep breath before blowing it out. "Okay, I'm not going to panic. Does the television work?" she asked, pointing to the seventy-inch encased unit.

Calvin laughed, "We are not that far from civilization. There's a satellite dish. You'll find more channels than you need." He looked at his watch. "Let me get going before the store closes."

He kissed her forehead and dashed out the door. He got into his Range Rover and drove two minutes down the road before backtracking to the other house only 300 yards away from the house he had left his wife in. He opened the door with his keys to find Julissa waiting on the bearskin rug by the fireplace dressed in a negligee and sipping on champagne.

"Man, I see I'm right on time," Calvin said as he took in Julissa's seductive beauty. He quickly began peeling his clothes off and placed them on a chaise lounge.

"Funny, I was wondering what was taking so long. And why are you stripping as if you're about to do a 'wham-bam-thank-you-ma'am' on me? I didn't drive all the way up here for you to hit it and run. Hell, we could do that in the garage of your house when the little Chihuahua goes to sleep, like we normally do."

"Julissa, please don't start. I'm trying, okay? Do you know how difficult this charade is for me? If you didn't pull that silly stunt of showing up at my wedding, I could have eventually introduced you to Michelle and I could have found a reason to have you at the house more often."

"So how much time do I get with my chocolate god? You know I'm getting excited just looking at that monster," Julissa said, licking her lips and nibbling on her long fingernail.

"That's what I like to hear. I told her I should be back in about an hour. That gives me plenty of time to devour these beauties." He joined Julissa on the floor and removed the negligee from her breasts. He took one nipple into his mouth and the other breast into his hand.

"Hmm, that feels so good, Big Daddy." She massaged Calvin's swollen cock before bending to take it into her mouth.

Calvin turned his body so he could free Julissa's package from the lingerie and began to suck while Julissa serviced him. They sucked, slurped, slobbered, and moaned as they pleasured each other on the bearskin. Calvin stopped Julissa and turned her on her knees as he entered her hole. "Ugh!" he yelled out as the wonderful sensation shot through his body.

"Fuck this pussy, Big Daddy!" Julissa commanded.

Calvin took pleasure watching his dick go in and out with each slow and deliberate stroke.

"Fuck it, baby! Fuck it!" Julissa yelled. "Ooh that feels so good, Daddy. Ay!" she cried out through short breaths.

Calvin pressed his sweaty chest onto Julissa's arched back, giving him access to squeeze her large, manufactured breasts. Twenty minutes later, he was exploding inside of her. He fell onto his back as he tried to catch his breath. Julissa lay on her side beside him with one leg draped across his legs and one of her breasts resting on his heaving chest as their tongues locked with one another.

"Baby, stay here with me tonight. Tell that bitch your car broke down or something and you couldn't get a phone signal to call with."

Calvin thought on the suggestion. "That's not going to work. She'll come knocking on this door before long. Can't have that happen."

Julissa pouted.

"I said I can't do that, Julissa. Stop acting like you don't know what's going on," Calvin snapped as he sat up.

"Well, at least allow me to return the favor before you go. You know I need my chocolate god completely satisfied," she said, running her nails between Calvin's thighs, massaging him along the way. Calvin instinctively lay down, turning on his side with his back to Julissa. She slid her hard dick into Calvin's hole after prepping it with some kisses. It felt so painfully good to him, that he wanted to cry. When Julissa was ready to release, she returned Calvin to his back, straddled his face, and let go into his mouth.

The pair cuddled with one another as Calvin dozed off and Julissa slyly watched him. Two hours had passed before Calvin awoke and found Julissa asleep next to him. He looked at his watch and realized that almost three hours had gone by since he had left his wife.

"Oh my god! Julissa, wake up!" he yelled as he quickly scrambled for his clothes. "Did you get the box of supplies I told you to get? I can't go back empty-handed, and I've been gone for three hours. I'm sure she's in panic mode by now."

"Calm down! I'm sure the miniature pit bull is just fine. The supplies are in the box near the door."

Julissa walked Calvin to the door. He picked up the box of supplies and then passionately kissed Julissa before hurrying out of the door. He quickly threw the supplies in the seat behind his and took off. As he drove the two minutes, he continued to hear an unusual noise that stopped once he stopped in front of his house. He grabbed his box of supplies and ran in the house to find his sobbing wife.

"Baby, what's the matter? Why are you crying? I'm sorry I took so long. The general store was closed, so I went a little farther out, and then I got to running my mouth, because you know that's how I make my money, and lost track of the time." Calvin went to join Michelle on the sofa to console her.

"Eww! You smell! Ugh!" she said, pulling away from him. "That smell is making me sick. It smells like a combination of perfume and funk."

Calvin laughed. "Oh yeah, I didn't tell you, I think I got sprayed by a skunk just before I got back in the car. When I saw it, I tried to scare it away and it sprayed before running away."

"Ugh! That's nasty," she said, laughing as she wiped her tears away. "Remind me to say 'no' the next time you suggest a trip to the mountains again. The whole time you were gone, I kept hearing noises outside. I tried to call you a few times, but I couldn't get a signal on my phone."

"Yeah, I worried about that. I tried to call, but wasn't able to get a signal either," he lied. "You would think paying seven-hundred dollars for a phone these days would mean something. I know the phone I lost the other day would have worked. I wish I would have bought the same phone instead of this newer phone. It's a piece of junk." Calvin inhaled deeply. "Uhm, is that my favorite Jambalaya I smell? Louisiana-style?"

"I don't know how you could smell it over that stinky skunk smell. Please go take a shower or something. And I see you stopped for ice cream before coming home."

Calvin was confused as Michelle wiped around his mouth.

"What ice cream?"

"It's all dried up around your mouth. Vanilla ice cream. So don't even try to deny it. You're busted. I'd lick it off for you if you didn't smell so horrible. And hurry off of the sofa before you leave that odor on it. Maybe after you're good and clean, I'll come join you in the shower."

"Oh no, no, no, woman! I'm trying to hurry up and get some of that good ole Jambalaya. If you come in the shower, it'll be time for breakfast by the time I get it." Calvin laughed.

"I don't mind," Michelle answered sheepishly.

"The next one. I promise," he said, pecking her on the lips before taking off for the bathroom.

15

Michelle

"Ahhhh!!!!" Michelle screamed as soon as she stepped outside the cabin to take in some fresh air.

Calvin bolted from the bedroom with just a sheet wrapped around his waist. "What's the matter?" he asked when he saw she was visibly shaken.

Michelle pointed to the trail of blood leading up to the headless rabbit. "Oh my God! Oh my God! Not again," she wailed out, clutching her stomach with her eyes fixated on the carcass. "Calvin, I can't take this anymore. I want to go home. I want to go home," she repeated.

"Honey, calm down. You're overreacting. We're in the mountains. There are plenty of wild rabbits around," he said, embracing her and bringing her back inside the house.

"That's a dead rabbit. Its head was missing. Just like the one in my car. Someone is here watching me, Calvin. They must have followed us here," she said as her heart raced. "I knew I heard somebody outside last night while you were gone."

"Baby, calm down. No one followed us here. Trust me, I would have seen them in my rearview mirror at some point as we drove that long, deserted road. It was most likely some animals you heard. Could have been a fox that caught the rabbit. It happens all the time."

Michelle beat Calvin in the chest, still hysterical. "You brought me up here with wild animals and vicious foxes that kill rabbits right near the doorstep? Are you crazy? Get me out of here now, Calvin!" she yelled, pushing away from him. "I can't take this. Get me out of here now!"

"Okay, fine. How about we check in at the inn twenty minutes down the road? That way we could salvage the rest of the weekend. There's more people around and plenty of tourists there. How about it?"

"Why can't we just go home? I want to go home. This whole thing is freaking me out. I don't want to be here any longer. Get me back to Atlanta where it's safe."

Calvin was frustrated. "Honey, your car window was broken twice in the same week. I wanted us to get away for a little R and R. If we go back home, you know I'll be tempted to work. I just need for us to get away for a while. The mountain here helps me to relax. I really do need this."

"Fine!" she conceded. "But we need to find a hotel that's not in the woods or in the middle of nowhere."

"You'll like the inn. It's very cozy. It has lots of charm and there's plenty of cement surrounding the place. There's also a nice restaurant there that we could have dinner at. It's only five minutes to the general town. I think you'll love it."

Michelle was already packed by the time Calvin finished talking. "Let's go! I want to get out of here," she demanded.

"Geesh, can I take a quick shower and throw on some clothes?" He chuckled.

"Shower when you get there, Calvin. Right now, I want out of here."

"Fine," Calvin answered annoyed as he threw on some clothes and went around collecting his belongings. "I have to get this place straightened up before we leave. I don't want to leave a bed full of cum and the kitchen and bathroom a mess."

"Whatever! Just hurry. Give me the keys so I can start loading the truck."

Calvin took a deep breath trying to contain his growing anger. "Michelle, would you calm down? It's seven-thirty in the morning. Would you stop it?

You're making my head hurt right now. Let's just get this place straightened up and I will load the car. You don't need to be lifting any heavy stuff. You take care of the kitchen and I'll do everything else. Just settle down, for crying out loud."

Michelle did as she was instructed without speaking another word. The last thing she wanted was to have her husband angry at her again. As Calvin cleaned, she continued to cause herself further anxiety by repeatedly looking out of the window at the blood from the dead rabbit. She stressed herself to cry in silence.

Despite Calvin's explanation for the dead rabbit, she knew there had to be a connection to the first dead rabbit. She thought of the rabbit being symbolic to the pregnancy, but since no one other than her doctor and husband knew about the baby, she dismissed the notion of there being a connection. She thought back to Angie's words a few days prior about Calvin possibly being the one to creep her out. No one else knew they were going to be at the mountain and yet he was hell bent on staying.

She checked her phone again for a signal when she thought about calling Angie to at least let someone know where she was, just in case her husband did turn out to be some deranged killer. There still was no signal on the phone.

When Calvin was done washing and drying the bedding and the bathroom was all cleaned, he grabbed their bags to take to the car.

"Aw shit!" he yelled from outside.

Michelle ran out to see what the new problem was. "What's wrong?"

"My passenger back tire is flat. I thought I heard something last night when I was driving back, but then I forgot about it."

Michelle began crying again. "I told you someone was out here."

"Michelle! Would you please? I have a spare tire so it's no big deal. I think if someone was out to get us, they could have easily gotten us and they would have flattened more than one tire. Don't you think?"

As arrogantly as Calvin posed the question "don't you think?" Michelle wondered if it was an insult or just looking for affirmation. She chose not to respond. She just wanted to get out of there quickly and didn't want to upset Calvin just in case he was a deranged murderer. She made a mental note to do a bit more digging into his background once her feet were firmly planted back in Atlanta. She was so head over heels in love with the idea of being someone's wife and a mother that she didn't take time to get to know who that someone really was. What Calvin did to his own best friend called his character into question.

While Calvin worked on the tire, Michelle noticed the tire tracks on the ground that the flat tire obviously made as he drove back to the house the night before. She walked far enough to provide herself a visual trail that took him from the house only 300 yards away.

"Michelle!" Calvin called out to her from under the car. "Where are you going? Don't go anywhere. I'm almost done."

"I'm not going far. I was just trying to see the scenery better," she lied.

She wanted to follow the path of the tire mark to the door of the other house. She saw a black Range Rover parked there that was identical to the one they were driving. She stared at it and noticed the details were very much the same as their car, down to the Georgia tags.

Movement from the smaller house caught her peripheral eye, directing her attention to the window. She noticed a tall brunette white woman looking out of the window topless. The woman didn't budge as she watched Michelle watching her. Michelle hadn't noticed Calvin walk up on her. He was more pleasant as he swooped her up by the waist.

"Come on, baby. I guess you were so engrossed with the spectacular scenery that you didn't hear me calling you. The car is ready and we can go now."

Calvin's eyes avoided the topless woman that moved from the window.

"Did you see that?" Michelle asked. "That bitch was standing in the window with her tits hanging out. Some people have no class. Hell, I was just going to say what good taste she has since her Rover is identical to ours. Same everything."

"I don't need to see someone else's ta-tas when I have a beautiful pair to wake up to every morning," Calvin said, quickly whisking his wife to the car as he repeatedly looked back.

"Are you okay?" Michelle asked.

"Uh, yeah. I'm just getting hungry. Maybe my sugar is getting too low or something. Let's just hurry so we can go and eat."

Not ten minutes after having breakfast and then checking into their room at the inn, Calvin started patting himself down. "Aw shit! I left my phone at the house. You want to go ahead and get some rest while I run back up there really quick?"

"Why don't I just ride up with you? Michelle asked, still suspicious from the flat tire incident and the woman in the window.

"Absolutely not! Not after all the hell you gave me to rush out of there without even getting a shower. I wouldn't have left it if I hadn't been rushing," he snapped. "No, you stay your butt right here where it's safe for you. I'll be back shortly."

"Okay. If you say so," Michelle sarcastically answered, rolling her eyes. She so badly wanted to tell him what she suspected, but figured she'd wait until they were back in Atlanta before broaching that confrontation.

"What's that supposed to mean, Michelle?" He looked at her as if he would kick her ass if she didn't let the subject go.

"Nothing, Calvin. Just go and hurry back this time," Michelle said, trying to soften her tone.

Still, Calvin took it to another level. "You know, I don't have time for this shit. Here I try to bring you on a romantic getaway and instead you want to get all bent out of shape about nothing. All of a sudden you're telling me—a grown-ass man—to hurry up. I'll tell you what, I'll be at the house watching television until we've both had enough time to cool off and think about this. This marriage means too much to me to start having silly arguments and throwing it all away. I'd rather us just have a few minutes apart until we can both fully appreciate the magnitude here."

Michelle's eyes filled with tears. She could hardly believe what she was hearing. She knew in her gut that there was more to this than was being said.

"Good lord, woman! What are you crying about now? I said I'd be right back and you get all bent out of shape wanting to treat me like some small child, telling me to hurry up. Now all I said was that I will be at the house watching television for a little bit so things don't get out of hand. You're not going to always get your way, Michelle. And I tried to make a concession by coming to spend a night in this rinky-dink inn as opposed to staying in that beautiful, spacious house. I needed to come here this weekend to get away from everything back in Atlanta, but did that mean shit to you? I didn't want to leave the cabin, you did. Coming here was a compromise. Can I please have just a few moments of peace in the house that I had to pay for?"

Michelle tried to mask her hurt, suspicions, and frustrations with all that was happening. "You're right. I'm sorry. I messed up this getaway with my foolishness. It won't happen again. Take your time. Relax yourself."

"Now that's the beautiful woman I married," he said with a smile, then kissing her forehead. "I won't be long."

As quickly as the door closed behind him, she broke down crying. After she collected herself, she called and left a message on Angie's voicemail saying where she was and talking about the dead rabbit driving her from the beautiful house to the inn she was camped out and waiting in.

Five hours went by before Calvin returned. He claimed he fell asleep while watching college football.

16

Angie

Angie sat and stared at the invitation Michelle had given her, along with her resignation from the talk show that the two formed together. It was like a slap in the face, but one Angie knew was inevitable with the addition of Calvin in their lives.

Angie wanted to call Michelle immediately to share the findings David called her about, but upon his request to hold out for the right time, she said nothing. They had set up a nanny-cam in Calvin's guest house and obtained more information than they bargained for. Angie was regretful that she allowed David to keep the footage with him after they returned to his house for a lovemaking session. Despite video being Angie's specialty, David said he would compile the data into one video. The feeling was like robbing a bank with someone and trusting them to hold the money.

If Angie had the video, she could have shown Michelle right away that Calvin was cheating on her. Life had become more complicated as her feelings for David continued to grow. Her loyalties were torn. Although David's presence somewhat pushed being back with Michelle out of her system, Michelle was still her best friend—though it seemed as if Michelle had forgotten that.

Lately, Michelle had pretty much made their relationship strictly business. Michelle went as far as telling Angie to stay out of her personal business and just do the job she was paid to do.

Angie was also growing weary of keeping her relationship with David a secret since they had grown so close, and in a nutshell, were partners in crime. She was also tired of trying to get Michelle all freaked out.

In addition to the rabbit left outside of the house in Tennessee, Angie had one delivered to the studio and graciously opened the box for Michelle when she was too freaked out to open the strange package herself. In an unrelated incident, Michelle's car windows were broken out again in addition to her tires being all flattened. When Angie asked David, he said he knew nothing about it. Apparently, Michelle had yet another person wreaking havoc in her life.

When Angie reluctantly arrived at the restaurant for the mysterious dinner party, she was ready to turn around the minute she spotted Calvin's family there. She wanted to go with David, but he felt it was best they showed no signs of involvement with one another, to keep anyone from getting suspicious when he exposed Calvin's secret to the firm. She agreed.

"Hmm, there's the skanky dyke now," Calvin's sister Tiffany immediately started, saying to her sister.

Angie rolled her eyes and shook her head as she walked past them, ignoring the comment.

"Did she just roll her eyes at us? She must not know who she's fucking with. She don't know I'll knock those eyes out of her head and kick the pussy out of her dyke ass, and she ain't gotta worry about nobody sucking her shit no mo'. She's probably mad that we don't want her dumb ass. Bitch!"

When Angie found Michelle, she said, "Michelle, you should have told me you were inviting the hood pack so I could have stayed home. I don't have time for this nonsense. That's *your* new family. I don't have to put up with their shit."

"Angie, please. Just ignore them. I want you here. I have a big announcement to make, and I want you to hear it first from me," Michelle said with pleading eyes, holding onto Angie's hands.

"Gee, the resignation and end to my career wasn't big enough? I can't imagine it getting any bigger than that," Angie replied sarcastically, pulling her hands away.

"Calvin was right about you. You were never my friend. You've only been acting like my friend just to have a job." Michelle waved her hand dismissively. "You know what? You can just leave. You probably would never be happy for me anyhow."

Angie was shocked by Michelle's curt words. She was angrier with herself for being in love with the woman for so long. "You know, Michelle, you're being very foolish right now and I'm going to pretend you never said that. When your whole world comes crashing down on you—and it will—I'll still be here for you. But as for tonight, I think it's time for me to make my exit. I'm a little too old for the drama you choose to surround yourself with. Have a good night." Angie turned to leave.

"Angie, wait!" Michelle called out as she followed behind her.

"No, Michelle. Not this time. You're on your own."

"Angie, I'm pregnant. I'm about to have a baby. I want you to be happy for me. That's why I invited everyone here together so I could announce it one time. That's why I'm resigning from the show as well. I've been under a lot of stress and we don't want to jeopardize the baby. You can understand, can't you?"

Angie stared at Michelle before responding. "No, Michelle, I don't understand. I don't understand how you can question my friendship to you while you keep something like this from me. Then want to insult my intelligence and lie to me each time I asked you. Then you put me on the same level with the hood rat family and want to tell me along with them. You don't even like them and they don't like you. And no, Michelle, I don't get how you put that man, whom you know nothing about, in front of our friendship. Also, you are correct in saying that I would never be happy for you. I've been your biggest cheerleader forever and out of our friendship, I have listened to your dreams and helped them come to fruition. You are who you are because of what I have sacrificed to make you. Talk show hosts come a dime a dozen. Everyone wants to have their own talk show. The big difference is they didn't have me in their corner. So you go on living in your fantasy bubble until it pops like every other bubble. Now if you'll excuse me, I have my own life to attend to."

Angie walked off without looking back as the tears filled her eyes. Her twelve-year friendship coming to an end was hard enough, but to see David watching from a distance and not running behind her made it more difficult.

She left to find a gay bar to drown her sorrows and possibly find someone who would help her temporarily forget about David and Michelle.

17

Michelle

Michelle stayed in bed depressed for two weeks. Her big happy announcement was anything but happy.

Calvin's family disrespected Michelle, her mother, and her grandmother to no end at the dinner, and Calvin didn't do much to defend her. At one point, he had the nerve to laugh when one of the sisters called Michelle's mother an over-the-hill, child-molesting cougar who chases young boys straight out of kindergarten.

When Michelle stood to leave, then Calvin said, "Okay, you guys knock it off." After the dinner, he suggested that Michelle find a way to get along better with his family since they'd be around often once the baby was born. That thought alone caused Michelle to contemplate an abortion and a divorce.

She came to life when she saw the familiar number pop up on her ringing phone, although she was hoping Angie would return one of her twenty-four phone calls.

"Hello," she answered with a smile.

"Hey, my Shelly-Poo."

"Who is this?" she asked, already knowing. There was but one person that ever called her 'Shelly-Poo.'

"It hasn't been that long, has it? This is Tony."

"Tony? Why are you calling me? What do you want?" She tried to play annoyed, but inside she was happy to hear from him. She was just glad that Calvin had left that morning to meet with a client in Chicago. She knew he would have a fit if he found out her ex was calling her.

"I was just calling to see how you were doing. I heard they cancelled your show so I thought you could use a friendly ear right now," he answered.

Michelle laughed as she sat up in the bed. "Friendly? Tony, you dumped me to marry your white pregnant bitch on the side after all I did to support you and your dreams. I'd say you're anything but a friend."

"Ouch! I deserved that. And if it makes you feel any better, you'll be happy to know I got what I deserved. Karma is a mutha."

Michelle was intrigued. "Oh really? How's that?"

Tony exhaled loudly into the phone. "Let me see . . . . Where do I begin? First, my marriage didn't last. Second, I recently learned the kid wasn't even mine. Third, I got shot in the back and will be in a wheelchair for the rest of my life. I'm paralyzed from the waist down, so that means my faculties no longer work and I think my wife may have been the one who shot me, but I can't prove it. The police think it may have been an intruder that was surprised by my being home. Unfortunately, my memory of that time is too impaired, but last I remember, my wife was the one in that kitchen with me. She had an alibi for that time, which I think is bullshit too—"

Michelle cut him off once she found words to speak. "Oh my goodness, Tony. How are you coping with everything? And for the record, no one deserves any of what happened to you. I'm just thankful you're still alive."

"Trust me; I have my days when I wake up wishing I would have died that day. It ain't easy living like this and then to find out my shorty wasn't my shorty. And the crazy part of this is, when the DNA test came back saying the kid was not mine, she blamed you. Said it was your fault for making her cheat on me." He sadly chuckled.

"My fault? How does she figure? You cheated on me with her." Michelle stood up and started pacing at this point. "I am so sick of that nutty chick."

"She thinks you were buying me to make me stay with you and felt I didn't pay her enough attention, so she cheated to get back at me. The baby's father turned out to be one my boys who was down with me since grade school. He cheated on his wife to hit Daphne."

"Daphne?"

"That's my wife. Her name is Daphne."

"You know what my biggest problem has been with the whole situation?"

"What's that?"

"Why'd you have to pick a white woman?"

"Hell, cheating is cheating. You'd have to be a man to understand. I was wrong to you, black or white. You were good to me and for me. I'm not sure why I didn't just go on and marry you. My life would have been a lot less complicated."

Michelle sat back on the bed. "Oh my goodness! I've been having a lot of crazy shit happening to me lately, stressing me to no end and Angie thought maybe your wife was behind it, but I couldn't understand why suddenly she had a new ax to grind with me. It all makes sense now if the paternity issue just came out and she's mad at me about it."

"Damn! I'm sorry to hear. What sort of stuff?" Tony asked.

"Dead rabbits keep turning up, my windows are getting busted, my tires slashed. You name it, it's been happening. Now my husband doesn't want me working because it's stressing our baby—"

"Oh, congrats! I heard you got married. I didn't know you were expecting too. That was kind of quick. You sure it wasn't some kind of rebound thing?"

"Please! Don't flatter yourself," Michelle said, getting defensive. "For your information, well over a year had passed before I hooked up with my husband, and I have always wanted to be married and have children."

"So are you happy now that you've got it all?"

"Of course I am," she answered an octave higher.

"Shelly-Poo is lying," Tony sang. "You can be honest with me, Michelle. I know you too well. Five years together."

Michelle took a deep breath as she debated whether or not to open up to Tony. The truth was, she was dying to tell someone how miserable she was.

"Really Tony, I'm good. At times it's a struggle because he has such a demanding job and I have to compete for time. Other than that, we're great."

Her eyes formed tears as it hurt to lie about her miserable life and the fact that she was convinced that her husband was cheating on her with the woman she saw in Tennessee and that he had the nerve to do it right next door. And with the uncanny resemblance of the parked Range Rover to theirs, she believed he either purchased the vehicle for the woman or they were together when he purchased his.

"Michelle, are you crying?"

"No," she said, making it obvious she was.

"What's wrong with my Shelly-Poo? Surely your life can't be worse than mine."

Michelle felt comfort in Tony's pet name for her. She was still in love with Tony and felt if she was not pregnant, she'd leave Calvin and take Tony back in a heartbeat—broken dick and all. Her life was now complicated by the child that she had always dreamed to have.

"I believe my husband is having an affair with a white woman. Talk about déjà vu." She deliriously chuckled through her tears.

"Do you have proof or do you just suspect it? You know how y'all women are always accusing us."

"But you really were cheating on me," Michelle laughed while still crying. "So I guess that means my husband is cheating on me as well."

Tony laughed. "Now-now, Shelly-Poo. You know it's not fair to make one brother pay for the wrongs of another brother. True, I messed up, but I'm sure you're just worried that your husband is going to do what I did. Throw that mess out of the window unless you have some cold, hard facts."

Michelle shared the entire story from Tennessee with Tony.

"That sounds pretty damn compelling, but I could see him getting stuck for hours watching all the college ball games. That would be a really bold-ass move to take his wife and his mistress up to the mountains at the same time for y'all to bump heads. He could have just told you he had to go out of town on business, taken his mistress, and left you parked at home alone. I mean, that's the way to do it if you gonna do it. As for the truck being identical, that would have me wondering, along with the tire tracks. Everything else I'd just toss. But now that you're carrying ol' boy's seed, I have to ask. What if he *is* cheating on you and you have all the proof you could stand? Say you even caught them butt-naked in bed, slapping skin. Then what? Most women have all the proof and then nothing."

"I don't know, Tony. I haven't thought ahead that far. I'm trying not to think about it at all. I'm just trying to have a stress-free pregnancy and a healthy, happy baby. It just gets hard at times, having no one to talk to."

"What happened to your friend Angie?"

"We fell out because of her not accepting and respecting my marriage." Michelle paused. "Tony, I have to go. Someone's at my door. Thanks for calling."

"Well, call me anytime. The number is still the same."

When Michelle opened the door, it was like she was seeing a ghost. There she was—the woman from Tennessee, who turned out to be the same woman who crashed her wedding.

18

David

'm still shocked to see you here, David. I thought for sure they were only bringing the two candidates for partner to Chicago. I certainly didn't expect to see you in the running. I guess I slept on you, huh, bro?"

"Underestimated is more like it. See, your problem was you never thought I was good enough. You never thought much of me at all. For years you looked down on me, but I was thinking, since this partnership is pretty much mine and I know you would never respect me being your boss, how about you give some thought to leaving the firm and starting your own firm? It just makes sense."

"Aren't you full of yourself? I guess you forgot the senior partners want a married family man. That would be me." Calvin laughed. He took a sip of his scotch they were drinking in the hotel bar. "Perhaps you should consider starting your own firm once I am crowned king of this hill. And since you're my boy and all, I'll even throw my client rejects in your direction to help your business."

"What clients? Like the ones you tried to steal but couldn't hold your liquor long enough to secure?" David laughed.

Calvin's jaw tightened. "I was drugged. I don't know how or by whom, but I certainly wasn't drunk. And although I can't prove it, I'll always believe you were the one who stole my phone and briefcase. If I wasn't sure before, seeing your snake ass here in Chicago is pretty damn convincing. I guess you thought I'd somehow lose my clients and it would move you up the ranks. Pretty smooth move, but my clients love me and never would work with you."

"Unlike you, Calvin, I don't need to steal clients. I'm here, aren't I? Unmarried and all. How about I get the job done on my own good merits and don't feel the need to step on people to make shit happen?"

Calvin was visibly rattled by David's words. He finished off his drink, stood up, and threw two twenties on the bar. "To show no hard feelings, drinks are on me."

"You might want to hold onto those dollars, 'cause I can pretty much guarantee you're gonna need them more than I will. You're the one who likes to live all grand and large. I'd suggest you hold onto every penny you can. Especially with a baby on the way, Mr. Family Man. Remember, this is business. It's never personal, my friend. Isn't that what you said when you tried to steal my clients?"

"Did Michelle tell you that?"

David looked amused, but confused. "No, that would have been *your* arrogant ass that told me that the very next day when I asked you why."

"Yeah, whatever. Drinks are still on me," Calvin said as he began to walk away.

"Give Julissa my regards," David called out loud enough for Calvin to hear.

Calvin swung back around as if demon possessed. "What did you say?"

David looked at Calvin daringly. "Oh, did I say Julissa? I meant to say your wife, Michelle. I don't know how your mistress came to mind just then, Mr. Family Man."

Calvin got close enough to whisper to David, "You fuck with me and you're a dead man."

David held both his hands up. "Whoa! Now you're threatening me? Doesn't sound fitting for a partner. I wonder how the seniors would feel about having a partner who threatens people's lives. They probably wouldn't give a shit if you had a woman on the side, but to have a *Julissa*? Hmmm, that may not sit too well with them."

Calvin closed his eyes and tightened his jaw before walking off for good. David laughed to himself.

When David arrived back to his hotel room, he sent Angie an email letting her know that Calvin threatened to kill him for mentioning Julissa. He also sent the full video footage from Calvin's night in the guest house with Julissa. Although David abruptly stopped communicating and taking any of the many calls from Angie, he knew he couldn't trust anyone else with the information that the pair worked together to collect. Never in a million years did David expect to see what he saw on that video.

Even though Angie was aware that Calvin was sleeping with Julissa, David could not chance letting Angie know that Julissa was in fact born a man and still had the anatomy to prove it. Had Angie gotten wind of that, she would have put aside all of their hard work to warn Michelle. Instead, he had been avoiding Angie by telling her that he was busy with his job.

More recently, he stopped taking any calls from her. He knew that Angie fell in love with him and he had no interest in being in a relationship with a lesbian he'd never be able to trust to hang around her women friends. He felt it was best for them to sever ties to eliminate any trails back to him for all the rabbit killings and car vandalism. If he was going to become partner, he certainly didn't need a criminal record.

As quick as he hit the send button, Angie was calling his phone. He let it go to voicemail. When he listened to the message, he heard:

"David, what the hell is going on? Why haven't you taken any of my calls and now you send me an email saying Calvin's threatening to kill you? You need to call me and let me know what's going on. See, this is the bullshit I could have done without. This is just why my ass became a lesbian in the first place, because all of you men are cheating dogs that want to play games all day long. My ass was so busy trying to dig up the skeletons on my best friend's husband to be exposed, while I should have been paying closer attention to your skeletons. You know, I don't appreciate being played by you, David. I don't know why you bothered to send me this email about Calvin trying to kill you and then you ignore my call. Next time keep your damn problems to yourself. I have my own problems. David, talk to me. Tell me why you are doing this to me—to us. This is not cool, David. I haven't done anything to make you treat me this way, unless you were just using me . . . Yeah, now that I think about it, you *were* just using me. You *did* play me. But fuck you! Goodbye and I hope Calvin snaps your fool-ass head off. Jackass! And I hope you don't make partner. You and Calvin deserve each other."

He deleted the message.

Ten minutes later, Angie called again and again. David ignored each call. When he listened to the new voicemail, she said:

"Oh my god! David! I just saw this video. Julissa is really a man! I can't believe you didn't tell me all this time. How could you hold something like this and not tell me? I thought we were better than this. You wouldn't have thought about getting that nanny cam if I didn't suggest it. You're wrong, David. So now you see Calvin likes dicks and now you can go fuck each other because you're certainly acting like a little bitch right now. Bitch!"

Then she hung up.

David felt bad for using Angie the way he did, but there was way too much at stake, and he couldn't see letting the opportunity pass him by. Angie was nothing more than a pawn in his game.

While they were up in Tennessee, David felt a strong connection with Angie that he hadn't felt before. The adrenaline-pumping thrill that they had collectively indulged in was the thing that brought them together. He loved how Angie showed that she was a do-whatever-necessary-to-get-the-job-done type of woman. She was a quick thinker and could make things happen despite her outward introverted personality. Once Angie let her guard down, she was just a regular ol' chatterbox with no off switch, unless she was kissed.

David only had the idea of sitting in the dark woods, waiting, seeing what they could see, taking pictures, and be done. Angie suggested the nanny cam with a video feed connected to the guest house as well as monitor farther back in the trees that caught a perfect shot of Calvin sneaking from one house to the other and then Julissa spending the extra few hours with Calvin in the main house after he dropped Michelle off down the hill.

Although Angie possessed much more technical knowledge than David, he was certain to take control of the situation so he wasn't at Angie's mercy. After reviewing the footage, he was glad he did once he saw himself on the video monitor flattening Calvin's rear passenger tire. He quickly deleted out that part.

Angie was also on the same video killing the rabbit and smearing the blood outside. She wanted to leave the trail of blood leading up to the guest house, but there was not enough blood, so she just left the rabbit nearby for Michelle to see. With some doing and manipulating of the video, he was able to remove the parts of the video that implicated him in any crimes.

Angie continually asked to see the video, feeling she was better able to put it together from a technical standpoint, and David repeatedly found a way to put her off. She'd say, "Just give the video to me. I could have it all together in no time. You know this is my profession."

When he got tired of her pressuring him, he told her he accidentally wiped out the video. When she offered for him to bring everything to her because she knew how to retrieve lost data, he stopped taking her calls since he had run out of excuses.

He was certainly going to miss the sex with her, because he really did feel she was one of his better sexual experiences, if not the best. While they were camped out at the inn, awaiting the completion of the video footage to take Calvin down with, they shared a very romantic time there together, despite their mission. That Saturday evening when they came out of each other's flesh long enough to check up on the newlyweds, they were stunned to see Calvin and Michelle heading to the restaurant that David and Angie were about to head to. David was glad he listened to Angie's suggestion to rent an SUV instead of chancing Calvin or Michelle spotting one of their vehicles up in Tennessee.

They retreated back to their suite, ordered room service, and stayed put until Michelle and Calvin checked out 6:30 that next morning. When they reached the top of the mountain at 11:00 that morning, they were in time to catch Julissa's departure from the main house and not the guest house. They hid until she was gone and then retrieved all of the video equipment. David was sure to hold onto everything because he couldn't chance Angie betraying him due to her feeling sorry for Michelle. Instead, he turned out to be the betrayer, but he had a mission to accomplish and he couldn't afford any distractions.

He thought about trying to rekindle the sex with Angie once he made partner—if she was desperate enough to have him back between her legs—but for now, he had the presentation of a lifetime to prepare for. He and Calvin were the final two being considered for the partnership and the decision hinged on successfully selling one final account. Not just any account; there were a group of billionaire real estate developers that were gaining very unfavorable reviews due to their choice to displace low-income families around the country in order to erect their string of condos with office parks and high-end eateries and boutiques. As much as David despised their tactics, he knew that his skills were good enough to help him sell a book of matches to the devil and ice cubes to Eskimos. Even if he had to throw a few undeserving people under the bus, he would see to it, by any means necessary, that Calvin was not made partner. He would hold onto his trump card until after they found out who would be selected. If Calvin was selected, then David had every intention of producing the video. If Calvin was not chosen, there would be no need.

19

Angie

"Answer the damn phone already!" Angie yelled through the phone after her fifth attempt at calling Michelle. She knew the things she had done to her friend were despicable, but she felt it was in Michelle's best interest to not carry Calvin's child, and a miscarriage would have eased Michelle's conscience more than an abortion would have.

Angie forwarded the email file to Michelle, wanting her to see it as soon as possible. She tried to call Michelle to prepare her for what she was about to see, but she wasn't picking up. She decided she'd drive to Michelle's and be there with her when she watched it.

But her aching heart caused her to try David one more time, and one more time he sent the call to voicemail. She couldn't understand what went wrong. She felt like a teenager with David. The last time she remembered her feelings being so wide open for a man was when she actually was a teenager and fell hard for her son Romeo's father.

Pete was six years older than Angie and was a smooth talker who charmed the drawers off of her with his comedy. She wasn't old enough to go to any of the clubs, but he'd practice his comedy routine for hours in front of her, while she should have been doing school work. For her seventeenth birthday, he graciously impregnated her with their son. He waited until she turned seventeen because that was the legal age of consent in Georgia, and on her birthday, she was all too willing to give him what he had waited almost four months to have. No one could tell her that Peter Michaels, aka Pete Smooth, didn't love her and was only taking advantage of her youthful innocence.

A few weeks later, when she told him she was pregnant, he began ignoring all of her phone calls and emails and wouldn't answer his door when she'd show up at his house. She contemplated an abortion the day she showed up to his house and some young, gold-tooth, chocolate, blonde chick answered the door half naked. She was claiming to be Pete's fiancée and demanded that Angie leave Pete alone.

Surprisingly, when Romeo was born, Pete showed up to the hospital to give him the name Romeo and get a paternity test, and then he disappeared to the west coast to pursue an acting career. The most success he had at acting was when he convinced a struggling Angie that the money she was loaning him was for his Actors Guild dues, and not for the drug habit he'd picked up while living in L.A. Angie was more disgusted with herself for sleeping with him when he came to visit their son in her new apartment that she worked hard to get on her own, than she was for letting him con her out of the $600. In addition, he made off with the television she had saved up to buy. The $600 was the money she had saved for furniture. After that setback, she contemplated suicide and was ready to give up her child, school, and everything else she had worked hard for. The suicide hotline saved her life that time.

By the time Pete showed up again, professing to be a born-again Christian who saw the err of his ways, Michelle was there to talk Angie out of swallowing a bottle of Tylenol. Angie so desperately wanted to believe her son would have his father in his life, but when Pete made off with their son's piggy bank with around $200 in it, she learned that the Devil is a lie and Peter Michaels is his name.

Angie became physically sick from the stress for days and missed work and classes for an entire week. When Michelle skipped classes to stay and take care of her, their friendship went to a whole new level. Another month after that, the relationship became an experimental intimate relationship. After a while, the pair concluded that the relationship was built on a rebound and called it quits. Angie tried dating men to prove to herself that she really was not gay, but between the emotional damage caused by Pete and the enjoyable pleasure of being with Michelle, it wasn't long before she started hooking up with women instead of men.

Being with David was like déjà vu. His strong sense of humor sucked her right into his game. His touch caused her weakness and the sex was spellbinding. And, as with Pete, she couldn't figure out what she had done wrong to cause him to suddenly shut her down. After their time spent in Tennessee, no one could convince her that David didn't love her, just as she had fallen in love with him. She felt what they had was special compared to what Michelle had with Calvin.

Angie still wondered if Calvin ever told Michelle he loved her. But after seeing that video, there was no way he could love Michelle and be banging a trans right next door to his wife. She would go see Michelle and console her as Michelle had done so many years ago for her.

20

Michelle

ichelle wasn't sure why she swung the door open expecting it to be Calvin when she knew he was in Chicago. Instead, she found Angie standing with a sense of urgency.

"What the hell do you want?"

"Michelle, please let me in. I want to be here for you. I've been trying to call you before you watched the video. Obviously you've already watched it," Angie said, seeing Michelle's eyes swollen from crying. "I don't want you to be angry with me. It was for your own good. You needed to see what kind of snake you're married to."

"What video?" Michelle asked.

"The one I emailed to you about two hours ago. It was a very large file so hopefully it went through, but I've copied the file onto a DVD for you. You have to see it." Angie handed Michelle the DVD she made. "I'll stay with you while you watch it, but I've got to get you out of here right now. It's best you leave his faggot ass now while he's gone. You have no idea what that man is capable of. He's talking about killing people, Michelle. He's desperate. You've got to get out of here now."

Angie was trying to get past Michelle inside of the house, but Michelle blocked her entrance.

"Get the fuck away from my house—my husband's house. How dare you come here to trash-talk him. Leave!"

"Michelle, just hear me out. Look at the video for yourself," Angie pleaded.

"Angie, go away from here with your lies. Don't come here ever again." Michelle flung the DVD outside like a Frisbee. When Angie turned to look in its direction, Michelle slammed the large door shut.

Angie pressed on the doorbell and pounded on the door. Michelle sat on the floor behind the door crying. After a while, Angie gave up and left. The last thing Michelle heard her say was that she was leaving the DVD on the doorstep. When Angie was good and gone, Michelle cautiously opened the door to grab the DVD.

That was the second blow she had concerning her husband in less than three hours. At first she was feeling a warm and fuzzy feeling when speaking with Tony. She was still in love with him, but he had made such a mess of his life that going back wasn't an option, just as she had made a mess of her own life.

As soon as she spotted the woman at her door, she knew it meant trouble, just as it had the minute she stepped into the wedding reception. Calvin told her the woman was a former client. Maybe, but what Julissa told Michelle on that day made her out to be far from a client.

"You? What are you doing here?" Michelle asked when opening the door to Julissa.

Julissa spoke with a sultry huskiness that could be confused with seductive if you were a man. To Michelle, she came across as a man living in a woman's body, but she was beautiful and captivating. She was both intimidating and confident. Her make-up was flawless. She was much more confident than Michelle.

Julissa pushed her way past Michelle, walking in and through the house as if she owned it, or soon would.

"Okay, you little Chihuahua, your time is up. My man is about to make partner right now as we speak, and there's no need for him to keep up this charade. You've been quite helpful and have served your purpose, so now it's time for me to put your ass on notice. Consider this your eviction, bitch! You have got to go. Calvin and I are in love and have been together almost four years. You, my dear, are nothing more than a pawn in this game we call life."

Julissa plopped down onto the sofa and stretched her legs as a horrified Michelle stared at her speechless.

"You, my dear, are just a naïve little fool who wouldn't know common sense if it bit you in the ass. Yet you call yourself a relationship expert." Julissa laughed out loud and exaggerated. She rubbed the soft Italian leather that caressed her body. "Uhmm, this feels so good. Wow, this makes me think back to every wonderful moment Calvin and I made love right here. Come to think of it, there isn't a square inch in this house we hadn't made love. All over both of his cabins in Tennessee. In our condo a few miles from here. And my personal favorite was while we were in Maldives just a few months ago—you know, for your honeymoon," she said with a wicked smile as she caressed her body. "You, my dear, don't have what I have and will never be able to please him the way I do. That's why he doesn't take you anyplace without taking me. You stupid fool. And now that he's in Chicago making partner—which he and I will be there celebrating in a few hours—you, my dear, will be gone—finito. He'll have no more purpose for you. I just had to come and tell you myself to see the look on your pitiful face." Julissa loudly laughed again as Michelle stood with flooded eyes and her hand covering her mouth.

The more Julissa spoke, the more manly she sounded instead of sultry. "You're a man!" Michelle spat out.

"No, darling, I am very much a woman—with an added bonus. A bonus that you will never be able to provide." Julissa stood up. "Have your shit packed and gone before we return from Chicago. And you might want to abort that little bug-eyed alien you're carrying since I'm not much for playing step-mommy. Could you just imagine holding the little creature, it spits on me, and it'll probably drop from my hands like 'oops!'" Julissa demonstrated dropping the imaginary baby and then laughed again.

Michelle finally found her voice and courage. "Get the hell out of my home, you bitch!"

"No, honey, this is *my* home. You're the visitor. You just make sure you're gone before we get back. If you choose to hang around, then you'll get to watch me and my chocolate god make love for hours . . . as we did up in Tennessee while you sat all by your lonesome."

Michelle ran to the kitchen and grabbed the largest knife she could find. The gun Calvin purchased for her to keep for safety was upstairs in a box in the closet. When she returned to the living room, Julissa was gone. Michelle searched the house and could not find her. What she did find was a photo of Julissa and Calvin together on a beach somewhere looking like the picture of true love. Michelle crawled into the bed while holding the photo that represented her crumbling world and cried until the doorbell rang again.

She was half tempted to hop on a plane to go find Calvin herself, but she knew no good would come of it. Instead, she gathered up whatever information she could to take Calvin down if he was, in fact, playing with her life and their baby's life as Julissa had alluded.

21

Calvin

Julissa was just what Calvin needed after the stressful morning he'd had. He hated to admit it, but David's presentation was solid, and he regretted sleeping on the man. He kicked himself for wasting time and energy with Michelle when David was as single as they come. Many of the senior partners pretty much guaranteed Calvin the position, but to his surprise, he arrived in Chicago for his final presentation to find that David was his only competition. He was wishing he hadn't done all he could to place a wedge between his wife and her best friend. She might have been useful in finding out David's strategy.

He wondered just how much David knew about Julissa. After the time David told him that Julissa came to the office, causing a scene looking for him, Julissa later told him that she never went to the job and had only seen David at a distance on the occasions when she showed up in different places. He then figured David was just probing by throwing out Julissa's name because he knew about the relationship. Calvin figured had David *really* known, he would have gotten word back to Michelle somehow. And if that would have been the case, Michelle would have started acting crazy and messing up his plans for partner. Nothing really made sense.

He did feel bad for beating Julissa up after she told him she had no idea what she was accused of doing and that she had not done anything to jeopardize his chance to become a partner; otherwise she would not have sat back for his farce of a marriage.

After a wonderful night of lovemaking, Calvin ordered room service for him and Julissa.

As Calvin was feeding her, she said, "Baby, I can't wait until we have this forever. Tomorrow they'll announce you as a partner and we can finally be together out in the open and you could be rid of that mutt you've impregnated. And that David will get his if it's the last thing I do. How dare he try to go against my chocolate god?"

"Julissa, please! Things are not that simple. My wife is about to have a baby. I can't just pick up and leave her. My family—my mother is so excited about this baby—"

"WHAT?!" Julissa pushed away from the table and stood up. "You said your mother hates her. And I thought you said once you make partner that we'll be together?" Tears filled her eyes.

Calvin's eyes did not pay attention to Julissa's tears or words. He was focused on her fabulous body that became exposed from the robe opening when she stood up.

"Calvin, are you hearing me?" She looked down to see where his eyes and attention were fixated and then closed the robe. "Now do I have your attention? You promised me, Calvin. Are you now going back on your word? Instead of playing that bitch, have you been playing me?"

Calvin stood from the table and took Julissa in his arms, trying to smooth talk her since he wanted more of her loving. "Baby, you have to trust me and let me work everything out. I can only deal with one thing at a time. Let me get through getting this partnership on lock and then I can focus on how to deal with the situation. I may not be excited with the mother, but I am looking forward to holding my very own child. I had never really felt what I felt until this. It's been really exciting watching the baby's progress."

Julissa pulled away from his arms. "So you have no intentions on leaving the bitch, do you?"

"Would you calm down? I don't need this added drama right now. I said just let me get things all squared. Just relax and trust me," he said, standing behind Julissa, massaging her shoulders as his erection started to come to life. His hands slid around her to caress her breasts. He planted light kisses on her long neck. She tilted her head as her tense body finally relaxed.

"Uhm . . . that feels so good—" she stepped away from Calvin and turned to face him with her robe still open—"but if you think you'll touch this ever again while that creature from the Black Lagoon is still laying in what should be *our* bed, in *our* home, you have another thing coming. I will NOT continue to be in the shadow, Calvin. I have helped you get this partnership and I'll be damned if I will accept second chair to a Chihuahua any longer."

Calvin threw his hands up. "You know what? Go! Just go! If you want to stand here and act like a simple bitch, then just get the fuck out of here. I told you I don't need this bullshit right now. They haven't made me partner yet and you're sitting here acting stupid. At least my wife doesn't give me any difficulty or act stupid. I really could do without the drama, Julissa, so get! Get on with your foolishness!" He dismissively waved his hands and started to head for the bedroom.

Julissa's tears flowed as Calvin's words pierced her heart. Before he could make it to the room, she yelled out, "Calvin, why are you doing this to us? I thought the whole purpose of my coming here was so we could celebrate your partnership and then we could finally go home and be together?"

"Home? What home are you talking about? Atlanta?"

"Your house. Our house!" she yelled out from behind the tissue as she wiped the snot from her nose.

"Our house? When the hell did MY house become OUR house?" Calvin yelled, laughing. "And don't forget, that cushy little condo you're in is mine as well. It's just a loaner to you—for now."

"What? What are you trying to say here, Calvin?" Julissa stood with one hand on her hip and a finger in the air. Her tears were quickly replaced with wrath. "So now I'm some replaceable, fly-by-night bitch to you?"

"Julissa, just get your shit and get out. Take your silly ass back to Atlanta. You can take that bullshit to somebody else, but I am not the one," Calvin said, walking farther away from Julissa, as he could feel his temper flaring.

"Fuck it! I could have many big black dicks that want this pussy. I have my own money and I don't need your shit or your Chihuahua-diseased dick."

Calvin turned back, rushed up on Julissa, and in one fluid motion, backhanded her just beneath her eye. She fell down on the floor, causing her robe to come undone.

"You want to fuck with me, bitch? Huh? You want to fuck with me?"

He got down on the floor on top of Julissa, pushing her leg in the air as he forced his way into her rectum and squeezed her silicone breasts as if trying to rupture them. When Julissa yelled out from the pain, he slapped her face again. "Shut up, bitch! This is how you want it? You want to play fucking games with me, bitch? Do you know who the fuck I am?" he yelled as he thrust harder inside of her. Julissa tried to contain her screams as Calvin tried to inflict greater physical pain.

Calvin stopped mid-stroke, getting up and leaving Julissa on the floor in pain. "Get your ass up and get the fuck out of here!" he yelled, acting as if he was about to kick her while she still lay on the floor. "And don't you ever tell me what you will or won't do. Do you understand me?"

Julissa tried to scoot back and away from Calvin's foot.

"I said, do you hear me, you bitch?!" Calvin repeated, moving closer to a cornered Julissa.

"Yes!" she said from behind her shielded face.

Calvin looked upon a frightened Julissa and felt remorse. He held out his hand to help her up, but she pushed it away. He was about to fly into a fit of rage, but didn't.

"Baby, get up. I'm sorry. I love you, but I just need for you to calm yourself and learn how to trust me," he said, squatting in front of her.

"Leave me alone! I hate you!" she cried out.

Calvin laughed as he took Julissa's face into his two hands. He kissed her forehead. "You don't mean that. Come on, get up so we can get showered and out of here. I have to see what Ole David is up to, that sneaky bastard. I'm sure he's probably schmoozing with the partners over breakfast."

Calvin helped Julissa up from the floor and then kissed her as if nothing was wrong. Calvin went into the bathroom to turn on the shower. "Come on, babe. We're gonna have to make this quick."

No answer.

"Baby, you hear me?" he yelled a little louder after stepping into the hot shower.

No answer.

"Julissa?"

No answer.

He stepped out of the shower he had just stepped into. "Julissa?!"

Still no answer.

He searched the suite and there was no sign of Julissa or her belongings. The robe she was wearing was also missing, leading him to believe she snuck out while still wearing it. He opened the door and peeped his head out. The housekeeping staff in the hallway looked at him frightened. Then he looked down to see where they were looking and he realized his ding-a-ling was dangling, causing him to quickly close the door. He punched the door, sending a sharp pain shooting up his arm.

"Shit!" he yelled.

He grabbed the phone to call Julissa. Julissa answered.

"Where the hell are you at? I was waiting for you in the shower."

"Leave me alone, you monster! You've hit me for the last time. You hurt me. You hurt me bad and now I'm going to hurt you back. I've been your fool for years. I'm done! I'll have all of my belongings out of your fucking condo tonight. I'm done 'borrowing' it. And I hope your baby dies, you sick bastard!"

And then the line went dead.

"Julissa? Julissa?" Calvin yelled through the phone before slamming it down.

He threw on some clothes and went downstairs to search for her, but was unable to find her. He went back to his room and packed to leave. He called the senior partners and lied to that his wife was in pain and he needed to get home quickly. They were very sympathetic, giving him a pass to leave. Calvin figured he'd catch up with Julissa at the airport.

22

David

"What the hell?" David yelled when he opened the door to his suite to leave for breakfast. "What are you doing here? How'd you find my room?"

"Please, you have to let me in. We have to talk."

David laughed. "I don't think so. You're not getting me into any shit. Take your ass from whence you came. We have nothing to talk about," he said, about to close his door.

"I could help you become partner."

"In case you didn't know it, I'm about to make partner without your help, so thanks, but no thanks."

"David, please! Please hear me out. I could give you any proof that you need. Calvin said you have been probing about who I am. He's been hiding me for the past four years. He only married that bitch to become partner. It's a charade," Julissa blabbed through her sobs.

"Janissa, Julissa, whatever the fuck your name is, I have your faggot asses butt-fucking, dick-slinging, and sucking nastiness all on video. I think that's all the proof I need. Trust me when I say, I have this partnership on lock, thanks to you." David laughed again.

"What!" Julissa's whole body language shifted. "You have us on video?"

"Oh-no! Get back, She-man. I already know you got a dick and I will drop your ass like the man you really are. I know you don't think your dumb ass is going to show up at my door thinking you wanna get froggy? I'm not the one. I'm not Calvin. I'll knock your ass out cold, you fuck with me," David laughed and then pointed to Julissa's bruised face. "You think those few bruises on your face is something? I'll leave your whole damn face swollen."

"Oh yeah?" Julissa challenged.

"Yeah!"

"We'll just see what the big boys have to say when I tell them you and I slept—"

Before Julissa could finish her sentence, she was going down for the count. David's fist caught her in the nose, knocking her out cold in one blow.

At first David's adrenaline was pumping high, "Yeah muthafucka! Now you know not to fuck with me. Come here to my motherfucking door talking shit. Well, who's talking now, bitch? I don't hear you talking now. If you didn't know, your bitch ass should have asked somebody, you fucking fag! Coming here with some bullshit! You knocked on the wrong fucking door today," he said, all hyped up.

However, as his loud voice caused people to peep their heads out of their doors to see what the commotion was all about, they found the half nude transsexual lying on the floor unconscious with the robe opening exposing the genitals. Everyone looked upon David with both disgust and confusion. David's anger quickly changed to panic when he saw Julissa's manhood peeking from beneath the robe.

"Oh hell no!" David yelled out. "I didn't touch his ass. He came here talking about falsely accusing me of messing with him. I was minding my own business on my way to breakfast, when 'it' showed up at my door."

"Someone call 9-1-1," one neighbor called out.

Damn! David thought to himself. *What kind of shit did I just step into?*

Hotel security showed up just as Julissa was coming to, totally disoriented.

"What's going on here?" one of the security asked.

"I was about to leave my room and found this she-man on the other side of my door threatening to tell people we slept together to keep me from being a partner, so her faggot-ass boyfriend staying upstairs could become partner."

"Well, did you?" another security officer asked.

"Huh? What? Did I what?" David asked. Surely they weren't asking what he thought.

"Did you sleep with her?"

"That ain't a damn her! That's a fucking man. Do I look like some homo guy going around looking for he-she's? Hell no! I don't even know this bitch."

"Enough with the name calling," the first security officer chastised. "Ma'am, do you want to press charges? Do you need medical attention?"

"What!" David yelled. "How are you going to ask 'it' if 'it' wants to press charges? How about you ask me if I want to press charges for 'it' coming here to threaten me and my livelihood?"

"You did assault her," the security responded.

"I defended myself. It came here to attack me and I defended myself."

"He raped me," Julissa said meekly from behind one of the security staff. "He beat me up and raped me."

By this time, there were six more security officers with two police officers and paramedics arriving. Without further question, David was pushed against the wall, handcuffed, and read his rights.

"You have got to be kidding me. This is some bullshit. I wouldn't touch that thing with a ten-foot pole. How are you going to just take that thing's word? Where is my justice? Hell, I want that she-man locked up for making a false report."

"Shut up!" a police officer commanded while slamming David against the wall again.

People applauded as David was carried away by the police, still fussing. Julissa went off with the paramedics.

23

Angie

O h no this trifling bastard didn't, Angie thought to herself after David's attorney identified herself.

"I don't know what David thinks I could contribute to his defense. Mr. Sneaky Man felt the need to eliminate me from his research after all the help I gave him. He wouldn't have anything if it weren't for me."

"Well, Ms. Lewis, that's what I need from you. I need for you to give me any information that you and my client were working on. Otherwise, Mr. Mosley will be facing a very long prison term."

"Why would I want to help his ass?" Angie screamed into the phone. "Let his ass rot for all I care. David is a trifling, sneaky-ass liar. I bet any amount of money that when you check those hotel video tapes, you will see that his sneaky ass probably was creeping with that trans. I'm not sure what you expect me to give you. David has the all the footage. He only emailed me a part of the file. He sent me enough to see that the 'she' we thought we were checking out was in fact a 'he.' I told David that was a man because she had too many manly features. David was hell-bent on getting proof so he could keep that other sneaky-ass jackass that married my best friend from becoming partner. I wanted proof so I could get my friend out of that farce of a marriage. Little good that did."

"Ms. Lewis, I have to ask," the attorney said apprehensively, "were you intimately involved with Mr. Mosley? You sound quite angry with him."

"First of all Miss, Miss—What was your name again?" Angie asked, ready to go off on the attorney for putting her on the spot with such a personal question.

"Talethia. Talethia Jacqueford."

"Well Miss Jackal—"

"No, it's Jacqueford. Jacqueford," she corrected, annoyed with Angie's blatant insult.

"Whatever! Anyhow, what I do with my personal life is hardly any of your damn business. Second, at this point, I couldn't give a rat's shit if they lock David up and throw away the key. And finally, I'd have to question your skill level as an attorney if you feel the need to call me in order to help your client. Personally, I would have started with the hotel cameras and his computer, which would document his trail. Now, since I don't get paid to do your damn job, but currently I *am* doing your job, I'm going to hang up now and do my own damn job. And tell David I hope he rots in hell!" Angie said before ending the call.

She could hardly contain the trembling from her anger long enough to hit "end" on her phone. A part of her wanted to go to Chicago to see David while he was cornered in a jail cell just so she could make him feel lower than he already was feeling—like how he made her feel. That would be the ultimate payback and it'd make her feel vindicated.

As she debated her next move, her doorbell rang. To her surprise, it was Michelle. She was glad Michelle was finally coming to her senses. *Obviously she must have watched the video*, Angie thought.

"Oh, Michelle." Angie opened the door with extended arms. "What you must be going through. I am here for you. I'm glad you know it."

Michelle stood outside of Angie's door looking at her strangely. Then she raised her hand to slap Angie's face, but Angie managed to catch her hand.

"What the hell is wrong with you? I try to help you and you come to my home to fight me? All I have ever done was try to be your friend, and you give me your ass to kiss? What's your problem?"

"What's my problem? What's my problem?" Michelle repeated, looking deranged. "You're my fucking problem! You are the low-life scum of the fucking earth, just as my husband continually said you were. You NEVER gave a shit about me. All you thought about was your-fucking-self. You evil bitch!" Michelle tried to swing on Angie, but Angie kept her restrained by the wrists.

"Look, I don't know what your fucking problem is, but I do know you better chill out with the hitting shit."

"Perhaps your dumb ass should have watched the damn video before giving it to me. I guess it was a good thing I was too shocked to turn the shit off."

"Huh? What the hell are you talking about? David emailed me that video and I sent it to you. And speaking of David, I just found out he's been locked up in Chicago because the he-she claimed David raped him in David's room. The lawyer just called me."

Michelle stood and stared at Angie. "So, you and David were in on this together, huh?"

"Michelle. I just wanted you to see what you were getting yourself involved with. Don't you understand that I love you and will always have your best interest at heart? You had to see that video for your own good—"

"Yeah, it was for my own good. I needed to see who was responsible for the knife in my back. To think, you have been terrorizing me all of this time, hanging around me as if you were trying to console me." Michelle shook her head repeatedly as she closed her eyes with a hurt smile on her lips. "You had me fooled real good, but I won't be your fool ever again. You go to hell and take David with you, you conniving bitch!" Michelle turned to leave in haste.

"Michelle! Michelle! What the hell? Michelle!" Angie called out, confused and hurt all over again.

Angie spent the next two hours trying to make heads or tails of Michelle's wrath toward her. Then she decided to watch the video David sent her, hoping to find some answer in it. She sat and watched every disgusting minute of the video, constantly forcing herself to sit through it all. Then finally she saw it. She saw David's ultimate betrayal that pushed her to take that flight up to Chicago.

24

Michelle

Michelle sat entranced watching the video again of her husband and the father of her baby making love to another man. She wouldn't have believed it had she not seen it with her own eyes. And even seeing it, she still didn't want to believe it was real. She wanted the tears to stop pouring from her eyes, but they would not. She needed someone to talk to and her mother seemed like the only choice.

"Honey, you need to just sit down and have a talk with your husband so he can explain himself. You can't be talking about running off half-cocked and pregnant. Believe me when I tell you, you're not going to want to raise any babies alone when you have a husband who is loving and supportive of you and the baby."

"Momma, he's with women with penises. That's not something I can just overlook."

"Well, fine! Leave the man and let some strange man help raise your kids and start tampering with them then!" her mother said in frustration as her voice cracked.

"Our own grandfather tampered with us—even you, his own daughter. Just because he's my husband doesn't make him exempt from being a child-molesting pervert," Michelle said, raising her voice and crying again.

"That man was NOT my father," her mother yelled back. "My mother left my father just because he cheated on her and traded my daddy in for a nasty man who loved little girls instead."

"What did you just say?" For the first time ever, Michelle was hearing that the man she always believed to be her grandfather was not. The man who everyone would tell her she was the spitting image of, was not her real grandfather. "How could you say something so cruel?"

"Cruel? You should be elated to know you weren't biologically tied to that man. That's the only solace I've ever had. All I'm saying is to sit down and talk to your husband. Give him a chance to redeem himself. You rushed into this marriage and now you're in it with a child. At the very least, you need to talk to the man. Get some explanation—"

"What's a good explanation, Momma? Huh? You tell me, exactly what explanation would justify my husband fucking another man?"

"Don't you speak to me in that tone! You made this mess and now you're looking for me to clean it up for you. If you have all the answers, what did you call me for? Take your baby and leave then, and just be by yourself. If that's what you want, then leave! I guess there's nothing left to talk about, is there?"

"Momma, I'm sor—Momma? Momma?"

The line was dead. On top of all else, she managed to alienate her own mother. Forgiving Angie would never be an option. She hated the fact that she had ever loved the woman. And in the snap of a finger, her had-it-all life quickly became have-nothing-and-nobody.

As messed up as he was, the man she had always known and loved as her grandfather, suddenly was not her grandfather. She wanted an explanation but then realized that under the circumstances, calling her grandmother to demand an explanation would offer very little in the wake of her current dilemma.

Michelle opted for the unthinkable. She resorted to doing something that she would have told any other woman never to do— snoop.

Snooping through Calvin's personal effects was going to be the only way she'd get to the bottom of the ugly truth about her husband. She went through his papers for over an hour, not finding much out of the ordinary. She did stumble across many sets of real estate papers for various properties Calvin owned. She even noted the one for a condo not too far from their home and remembered the other woman—man—saying something about a condo. Michelle wrote down the address. Finding a bra and an extra large thong, obviously belonging to the person who felt the need to barge in her home, was enough to send Michelle to go to the address she had written down.

Michelle was greeted by the doorman when she arrived in the luxurious building.

"Hi, may I help you?" the young and pleasant man who doubled as security asked.

"I'm looking for Calvin Edwards."

The unsuspecting man smiled. "Mr. Edwards left a short while ago. I believe he said he'd be back later this evening."

Michelle tried hard to contain her emotions and smiled, particularly since he was supposed to be in Chicago. "Oh. Well, is the lady of the house in? I'd love to speak with her if she's in."

He frowned. "Oh, strangely, Mrs. Edwards came in for a hot minute and asked if her had husband made it in, but then she left back out. She looked in very bad condition and said she had to run back out for a doctor's appointment."

"At night?" Michelle asked on the verge of tears. "What doctor's appointment did the bitch have at night?" she yelled out, unable to hide her emotions any longer.

The security officer looked at Michelle as he tried to figure her unstable behavior out. "Ma'am, I'm going to have to ask you to leave the premises now."

Michelle held her hands up as the security was about to put his hand on her to escort her out. "Don't you dare touch me! You tell Mr. Edwards when he returns that the real fucking Mrs. Edwards came by and you fucked up and confirmed that he has some bitch here on the side. Or better yet, how about

I tell my husband that you told me about his other bitch?" she yelled, as the security officer's face screamed panic.

"But . . . but . . . but I didn't tell you that. You asked for Mrs. Edwards."

"NO! No I didn't! I am Mrs. Edwards. I said 'the lady of the house' but you volunteered the 'Mrs. Edwards' bullshit. Well, I'll have you know, that dick-slinging bitch ain't even a fucking lady. She has a dick as big as Calvin's, and last I checked, women don't have dicks." Michelle dug into her purse and pulled out the DVD and handed it to the security.

He hesitantly took it from her. "What is this?"

"It's my gift to you. Do with it what you feel. I won't be needing it anymore. And when you're done with it, give it to my husband and tell him I said he better never come near me or my baby ever again. Tell him to stay here with his bitch or whatever the hell he calls it, but it damn sure ain't a fucking woman," Michelle said as she turned and left feeling temporarily empowered.

25

David

"Y ou are such a scum, David. Why would you have me blindsided like that? How come you couldn't tell me this was some random chick you were fucking? I am going to get you out of here, but you damn well better find yourself another attorney. I might find myself too tempted to cause you to lose this case."

David buried his face in his hands. He wasn't thinking when he had Talethia contact Angie to help get him out of jail and his name cleared. Talethia was another of those women he shut down communications with a couple of years ago, but when he ran into a delicious looking Talethia, who just happened to be a criminal defense attorney, in the hotel bar a few nights ago, he couldn't help but say everything he thought she wanted to hear for a moment inside her hot, wet cave. She had just left his room at five o'clock that morning. Naturally, she was his first and only phone call.

The deputies were talking about thirty years in jail for a rape he had not committed. For his freedom, he'd find a way to smooth things out between him and Angie. He'd even find a way to justify his betrayal. Part of his job was lying for a living to keep others from looking bad. Now he had to do whatever and say whatever to save himself.

"Talethia, she's a lesbian. She doesn't like men," David said with a nervous laugh.

"How stupid do you take me? That was the sound of a woman who is in love with you. One you are obviously fucking or maybe, you did her like you did me and spit her out when you were done getting all the flavor you could out of us. I bet that's how you do all women, don't you? I don't know what I was thinking crawling back into a bed with you," she said, starting to raise her voice and lose her professional demeanor.

"Sweetheart, please believe me. Calvin was my good friend and Angie is in love with Michelle. They've been best friends for twelve or so years, and at one point they were in a relationship. Michelle decided she wanted children and married Calvin in a matter of weeks. Both Angie and I objected and wanted to find a way to bust the relationship up, so we teamed up for that reason only. During the course of our investigation, we stumbled upon the she-man. At this point, I was in the running for partner at our firm. Then I found out Calvin was trying to steal my clients in order to make partner, though he had no idea he was competing against me for the spot. When Angie and I found out that Calvin and Michelle were heading to Tennessee, Angie wanted to keep an eye out for Michelle because she was worried about him doing something to her.

"We went up there, camped out, and set up video surveillance just in case anything happened so we'd have proof. Lo and behold, we found more than either of us expected. We both could clearly see that Calvin was cheating on his wife, but it wasn't until I saw the video that I realized it was really a man."

"Okay, that doesn't explain her reaction," Talethia said, still skeptical.

David pondered on what to say next. "At one point when we were sitting parked in the car, she told me she was going into the woods because she had to use the bathroom. I was a bit concerned because it was night and there might have been animals out there. She assured me that she'd be fine. However, once I watched the video tape, I realized she wasn't telling the truth. I wasn't sure what kind of game she was playing or had me roped into, so I decided to sever ties because I couldn't chance being a part of any criminal activities. I didn't need her blackmailing me or anything."

"For the record, setting up surveillance in someone's home without their permission is a crime, but go on."

David looked as if he were shocked. "Anyhow, up until the other night, I had never sent her a copy of the video. I only sent it when Calvin made a threat on my life. I'm sure she saw what showed up on the video and it caused her to become angry," David explained convincingly.

"What exactly is it that she has done that would cause her to become so upset?"

26

Angie

I 'd like to see David Mosley. I think he was brought in a day or so ago."

Angie stood patiently as one guard checked with another guard and they checked the paperwork before making phone calls. Then they had another discussion amongst themselves before finally returning to the thick Plexiglas window that visitors had to speak into a window microphone in order to communicate.

When she boarded the plane from Atlanta to Chicago, the bitter cold temperatures in Chicago had slipped her mind. When she stepped out of the airport and the wind whipped through her trench coat, she was even more determined that she'd make David suffer.

"I'm sorry, ma'am, Mr. Mosley was just released about an hour ago with his attorney."

Angie was ready to blow a gasket. "Ms. Jackalford?"

The guard looked into the computer. "Yep. Something like that. It's pronounced a little differently, though."

27

Calvin

W hat the hell are you doing here?" Calvin asked when he pulled up to his house to find Julissa about to leave.

Julissa had panic on her face. She held her hands up to shield herself. "Please don't hurt me, Calvin."

Calvin noted the blood clot in her blackened eye in addition to the bruising he caused. He grabbed one of her arms to move it for a better look. "What happened to you?"

"Your friend David. David did this to me and I had him locked up. I told the police that he raped me. I wanted to help you become partner," she lied.

Calvin chuckled. "Oh really? Where's he at now?"

"In jail. They said he'd get at least thirty years."

"Is that so?" Calvin asked, skeptical. "So what are you doing at my house—where my wife would be?"

"I needed for you to see what David did to me. If your wife came to the door, I would have just told her I was your client and it's an emergency, since you've already told her I was an international model."

"Is that so?" Calvin asked again, tightening his grip on Julissa's wrist. "Where's my wife?"

"No one answered," she replied, getting more nervous by the second as she tried to wiggle herself from his grip. She looked around the two acres wishing there was a nosey neighbor within eye- or earshot that she could scream out to for help and maybe make a run for it. Surely Calvin would catch her if she tried to run.

Calvin pulled Julissa back toward the house and unlocked the door. He pushed her inside as he called out for Michelle. There was no answer. He continued to pull Julissa, letting go of her arm in exchange for her hair.

"Where's my fucking wife, Julissa?"

"I don't know," she cried out, wishing like hell the woman she hated would show up to save her.

"My wife doesn't go out this time of night. Where the fuck is my wife at?"

"I swear I don't know. I had just got here when you pulled up," Julissa said at a higher pitch to refrain from screaming, as Calvin yanked her by the hair.

As Calvin's eyes surveyed for anything out of the ordinary, he noticed the gun he purchased for Michelle sitting on the table. He picked it up and saw that it was loaded.

"Why is my wife's gun sitting here? This tells me she must have been worried about something. And why would she go out this late without it? What have you done to her, Julissa?" Calvin asked through gritted teeth, as he shook Julissa's head like a rag doll. He then dragged her by the hair to the kitchen when he noticed blood on the door to the kitchen. "You better start talking real quick, bitch!"

He threw her on the floor and pointed the gun between her eyes.

"Please, please don't shoot me. I love you. I have not touched her. I swear," Julissa sobbed.

As Calvin kept the gun on Julissa, his eyes surveyed the rest of the kitchen. He noticed a photograph sitting on the island and he noticed more blood near it. Keeping the gun aimed toward Julissa, he went to pick up the picture. It was Julissa and Calvin together on a beach. He pointed in Julissa's direction. "Did you give this to my wife?"

"No!"

"Don't fucking lie to me. You had this picture in a frame on the nightstand in the condo. How did it get here?" he demanded, pushing the barrel of the gun into Julissa's wounded eye.

"Ow! You're hurting me!" she cried.

"I'm about to blow that eye out of your head if you don't start talking quickly."

"Okay! I didn't see her today. I came by before I flew to meet you in Chicago and told her to leave because I wanted us to be together and you said that once you made partner, we'd be together forever. I couldn't stand the waiting any longer. Calvin, we belong together. Please don't hurt me. She probably left because she was upset. I swear she was fine when I left the other day," Julissa spoke a mile a minute, pleading for her life.

"Why were you at my door when I pulled up?"

"I thought she was gone and I was looking for you to tell you that David won't become partner because I had him locked up for raping me."

"David raped you?"

"Uh… uhm… yes! Yes, he raped me," Julissa lied, hoping to gain an alliance with Calvin.

Calvin laughed as if a joke were told, lulling Julissa into a false sense of security. "Get up!" he told her as he laughed. "So they had to take you to the hospital and everything, right?"

"Yes, they did a full exam and said he'd be going away for at least thirty years. So I figured that automatically makes you a partner by default."

"You thought of everything, didn't you?" He continued to laugh while lowering the gun to his side. "Go upstairs and get undressed. I want you in the shower."

Julissa finally relaxed and smiled. "You're not angry with me anymore?"

"Julissa, you will always be Julissa and that won't ever change. Since I've known you, you have always been—you have always done things how Julissa wants. You have to love that crazy, witty side of you."

"Oh Calvin, I love you so much."

She ran over and kissed his lips and then started unbuttoning her shirt.

"Go ahead to the shower and get all clean. I'll see you up there in a minute. Don't use the bathroom that we normally use. I want you in one of the other bathrooms. Use the one at the far right side of the hall. The room with the waterbed. You like that room, right?

"Oh yeah!" Julissa said seductively, trying to keep her fear from her voice. She knew she needed to find a way back into Calvin's good graces so that she'd have enough time to flee him for good. Her shirt was fully opened and she unsnapped her bra, releasing the breasts that she knew Calvin loved.

He immediately began tasting them and rubbing them. "Go. Go on. Get cleaned up."

Julissa did as told. Calvin looked around some more to determine the whereabouts of his wife. He checked her closet and everything was intact. Then he went into the bathroom with Julissa. She still appeared frightened. Calvin looked upon her body as she stood in the opened shower.

"I was thinking about remodeling this bathroom. What do you think?" Calvin asked, looking around it. "What colors should I use in here?"

Julissa tried to relax. "I like it as it is. I love the warm green colors you've used. I say keep it."

"No, I'm thinking of something with splashes of red . . . like a blood red."

Julissa wrinkled her brows not liking the sound. Particularly since Calvin was still fully dressed and looking deranged.

"Aren't you going to get undressed and join me?"

"Nah, I think I'll just watch."

She became more nervous as Calvin's eyes seemed to pierce her. There was a sinister look in them.

"So what exactly happened when they took you to the hospital? They collected a few swabs, right?" he asked.

"Ye-yeah . . . yes," she stuttered, trying not to look at him but at the same time trying to keep him in view.

She reached for the knob, about to turn the shower off.

"Oh no, leave it on. Wash up again," he ordered. Julissa wouldn't argue. "So I take it they collected some DNA samples of David from your ass? Did they also swab your dick?"

Julissa shrugged her shoulders on the verge of tears. She knew at that point there would be no safe answer and lying wouldn't be an option with Calvin. "I think so."

"You think so? How do you 'think so'? Wouldn't you remember that shit?" he asked, becoming agitated. "Please answer that for me, Julissa."

"Calvin, I'm sorry," she blurted out, finally breaking down to cry. She got down on her knees in the shower. "Please, I'll do anything to make it all right again. Please just give me a chance," she begged with her hands pressed together.

"Julissa, you have made such a mess of my life. Every time I tell you to do something, you do the opposite. When I tell you not to go somewhere, you go. David's hotel room was on a different floor from mine. How could David have raped you AFTER you snuck out of my room? Did you go to his room, Julissa? Did you go there to tell him about us so you could hurt me? Did you? And did you come here today to try and get my wife to turn against me too? And when she wouldn't cooperate with you, you did something to her?"

"Calvin, I swear—"

Calvin took the back of his wrist and knocked Julissa in the nose, causing an instant gush of blood.

"Oh my god!" Julissa screamed as she looked into her hands and saw the pool of blood. When she looked back up, she looked directly into the barrel of the gun just as it went off.

"Damn! I think you were right. The red splatter doesn't look good in this bathroom. I guess I'll just clean it up and keep the warm earth-toned colors instead."

He laughed to Julissa as he looked at the splatter of her brains all over the shower. He let the hot water continue to run as he went to the garage to find something to dispose of her body. He found a large trash container and a saw. He brought them and some trash bags back into the bathroom with Julissa's corpse. He took off his clothes and got into the shower to remove the remainder of her head and placed it in a bag. He cut each of her limbs off and placed them in separate bags. He removed Julissa's penis and held it for a moment as he reminisced with a twisted smile before placing that in a bag also. He caressed her silicone breasts as he had so many times before, then cut them out before sawing her torso in half.

He got some cleaning supplies and scrubbed the evidence from the shower walls. When he was done, he dried himself off and carried Julissa's mutilated body down to the garage. He returned to the shower to wash himself off before getting dressed. He pulled Julissa's Range Rover into the garage and loaded the contents of the trash can into the back.

He headed back upstairs to make sure everything was in order. He replaced Michelle's cleaned-up gun on the table, then drove off in Julissa's truck identical to his own.

About 200 yards away from his Tennessee home, he opened each of the plastic bags containing the upper torso, the limbs, and the penis and laid them out for wild animals. The following morning, he burned Julissa's remains, along with the scraps left by the animals, in an outdoor container. He cried like a baby as he realized what his alter-ego had done. He didn't know how he would manage without Julissa. She had become a part of him, but when he thought of all of the mess she caused him—that he still had to deal with—he collected himself. He vowed that from that point on he had to focus on how to undo all the damage.

As he stood from the ground he fell on to cry, he realized something was missing. He didn't recall seeing Julissa's head amongst the carcass. He brushed himself off and went to look inside the car. There was nothing there. Panic gripped his bowels as he thought what would happen once Michelle found Julissa's mangled head, provided nothing was wrong with Michelle.

28

Michelle

ichelle pulled up just in time to catch Calvin pulling off from the house. She drove the two hundred plus miles in a blind rage. She didn't know what she'd do or say once she found him. She didn't even know why she was bothering herself to look for him. Once she opened the plastic bag left on the garage floor, she knew there was no way she'd leave him without letting him have it.

"You dirty, rotten son of a bitch!" she screamed while blocking his path from leaving. She got out of his Range Rover and made her way over to the identical Range Rover. She slammed her hand on the hood. "Get your ass out of there, you fucking homo! You fucking coward! And where's that bitch at? Baby or no baby, I will fuck his ass up— and yours too."

Calvin slowly got out of the car, not knowing what to expect. Michelle slapped his face so hard he saw stars. He grabbed her as she was continuing to swing on him. She sobbed so hard she collapsed onto the ground. Calvin stood watching her at first, but then got down on the ground to console her. She was about to fight him some more, but he held her tightly as he also cried.

"How could you do this to me?" she yelled. "How could you? Were you and Angie in on this the whole time? Is that why you wanted me to stay away from her?"

Calvin wrinkled his forehead in confusion but kept silent.

Michelle continued. "Why would you and Angie want to traumatize me like that? Why would you leave a dead animal in the middle of the garage floor? And don't try and deny it, because I know it was you. If you didn't want me to carry this baby, then why have me get pregnant? Why are the two of you trying to cause me to lose my baby? I guess I have David to thank for catching Angie on camera killing and smearing the dead rabbit out here. Also for letting me know my husband is gay. And why would you marry me if you wanted to be with that half man, half beast? She told me all about your relationship and how you planned on putting me out once you made partner. How could I be so stupid and blind?" Michelle broke down again, and then said, "I hate you! I hate you! I hate everything you stand for." She tried to fight him again, but he held onto her tightly, restricting her movement. "Get the fuck off of me!"

"Michelle, please. I'm sorry. I know I have hurt you, but I want to spend the rest of my life making it up to you. I was wrong, but I do love you, and I don't want to lose you or our baby. I'll do anything you want to fix this."

"Fix this? How can you fix this? How can you undo all of the damage you have caused me? Us? All you ever gave a damn about was making partner and you were willing to throw me under the bus just to have it. I trusted and believed in you and then you want to be in cahoots with my best friend to destroy me?"

Again Calvin was confused. "What are you talking about? I don't even talk to your friend. I never have unless you were around. I don't like her. I've always told you that. I knew she meant you no good."

"Then why would you leave that dead animal in the bag in the garage for me to find? I looked in the bag and saw the eyeball. It almost looked like a head or part of a face."

Calvin worked to contain the panic. "Sweetie, believe me, I didn't leave it intentionally. I saw a pair of jackals on the property and I killed them. I didn't realize until after I got up here that I left one of the bags. I was trying to get them as far away from you as possible. That's what I was up here burning."

Michelle looked as if the explanation was plausible. "How come I've never seen any animals around the house?"

"Baby, I don't want to scare you, but on occasion, all kinds of critters will roam around. It's rare, but it does happen from time to time."

"Why didn't you just call Animal Control to get them?"

"Because I didn't want you to know about them. I know how terrified you were about the rabbit situation—and by the way, what did you mean about Angie smearing the rabbit and it's on video?"

"While you were *supposed to be* in Chicago, Angie brought me the video with you and that thing having sex, right here. You had her— him—it right here. You had a man fucking you Calvin. How could you? And while I was right next door," she said, breaking down again.

"Michelle, I can't apologize enough. I promise you that chapter of my life is now closed forever. That was a phase I was going through, but when I met you, I didn't want to lose you. I just wasn't quite ready to let my secret life go either. Do you know what a blessing you are for me? And this baby—"

"Why, so you could become partner?"

"That was part of it at first, but right now I don't care about any of that anymore. While I was in Chicago, I realized how much I stood to lose by putting my selfishness in front of you and our baby. I told her then that I never wanted to see her again because I realized I was a married man in love with the best thing that could have happened to—"

Michelle turned to him, cutting him off again, and asked, "Then why were you at her condo waiting for her? Or should I say 'your' condo? Yeah, I know about that too. That's where you and 'Mrs. Edwards' live." She started crying again.

Calvin delayed his response by trying to console Michelle as he thought of his next lie. "I told her that she had to leave my condo. I did let her stay there since I was hardly ever there. But I have never told anyone that she was my wife. She must have done that. When I told her she had to leave, she threatened to burn the place down. I went there to make sure she wasn't doing what she threatened to do."

"Stop referring to that thing as a 'she!' It has a dick just like you have a dick. It's a fucking man with store-bought tits."

Calvin said nothing. Instead, he stood from the ground and held his hand out for Michelle. She swatted at his hand and struggled up from the cold ground on her own. Calvin walked to the main house and unlocked the door. Michelle followed, not sure why she was listening to anything Calvin had to say at that point.

"I want to know why you didn't tell me the truth about him. Why didn't you tell me you were involved with a fucking man for four years, Calvin?" Calvin looked at her surprised. "It came to the house while you were in Chicago and told me all about the two of you and how you were together on our honeymoon. He said that you only married me to become partner and now that you were, I had to 'be gone' by the time the two of you returned from Chicago. He said the two of you had sex all over that house. He said—"

"Michelle! Michelle, please stop! That's all done. I fucked up. I didn't see any way of telling you the truth about Julissa. Yes, I had been with her for about four years. I'm not sure why I stayed in that situation, but I know when I met you, you were the person I wanted to marry. I could have easily married her and no one would have been the wiser."

"Bullshit! The more she spoke, the more it was obvious that it was a man. You didn't want anyone to know you are gay. That's why you played this game with my life. Please tell me how you could think it is okay to be with both of us. Either you want to be with a man, or you want to be with a woman. There is no both of us."

"Michelle, I have no intentions of being with Julissa ever again. Not anyone other than my wife. I don't care if I don't make partner. Right now, fixing my marriage is the only thing important to me. I am about to have a son. I want to be a good father to our son. I want us to be good parents for our baby. Michelle, I love you and I always will. I love this little fella growing inside of you," Calvin said, rubbing her belly with a warm smile. Michelle almost smiled.

He continued. "You know I could say sorry a million times, but it will never right my wrongs. I was wrong. I should have severed ties with her the minute I met you. If I could change things, I would, but I can't. Instead of focusing on trying to be a partner, I am going to focus on my family—you and this baby are my family. You're all that matters to me now. Please . . . please give me a chance to make things up to you. Let me fix the damage I have caused you." Calvin cradled Michelle's face and wiped her newly escaped tears.

She closed her eyes as she felt herself melting, trying to make some sense of her life.

"I came here to catch you with that beast and I wanted to kill you both. You hurt me, Calvin. You hurt me bad. I don't know if I could ever forgive you. I'll always have to worry about her popping up and causing my life hell. Your family causes hell in my life and you let them. They make me hate carrying your child because of the life I'll have to endure with them." Michelle shook her head as she paced. "I can't do it. I can't."

"I will make sure they never disrespect you or your family ever again. I was wrong for not putting a stop to it in the first place. Michelle, I love you and will do anything for you and our baby. Just give me a chance."

"No! I can't. I can't just forget everything."

"I've decided to forfeit my chance to become a partner. I don't care about that anymore. I just care about you—us. You are my world, Michelle."

"No! Leave me alone!" she yelled when he started rubbing her shoulders. "And I don't want you in the house with me. Don't come back until I find someplace to move to. Stay at the condo with your freak. Just stay out of my life."

Michelle flew out the door and back to the car. After throwing things around the house, Calvin noticed Michelle's pocketbook on the chair and ran out as she was pulling off. He called out to her, but she would not stop. She made it all the way to a gas station in Georgia before she realized that she didn't have her cell phone or her pocketbook with the gun that she intended to shoot Calvin and his lover with.

29

Angie

've sat back for your bullshit long enough. I want you to get your ass out of Michelle's life now."

After failing to track down David in Chicago, Angie decided to drive to Calvin's house in Tennessee, also hoping to find him there with his lover. Instead, she found him looking distraught with the door wide open and the inside of the house in shambles. She nervously looked around the house, as Calvin hadn't even acknowledged her.

"What the hell is going on in here? Where's Michelle?" she asked when she spied her pocketbook. "What have you done with her, you trifling bastard?"

"She left," he answered, finally acknowledging her presence.

"Why is her pocketbook here? She wouldn't leave without it. What have you done with her?"

"I said she left!" he snapped. "And what's it to you? She told me you were the one leaving dead rabbits and traumatizing her. What kind of friend are you supposed to be?"

Angie looked shocked. She couldn't believe Michelle would tell Calvin, of all people, despite everything else in the video. "She told you that?"

"Yes, my wife told me. Why wouldn't she tell me? Her so-called best friend does everything she could to scare her half to death, vandalize her car not once, but three times, pretend she's being loving and supportive, and then think she has the right to question my motives. Why would she need enemies when she has you standing in her corner, pushing the knife in her back? I knew you were untrustworthy, which is why I told her to stay far away from you. She didn't want to accept that you'd do anything to hurt her, but thankfully, you have provided her with the video footage to not only keep you out of her life, but to have your ass locked up."

Angie's eyes grew wide as Calvin spoke. "First of all, I did not vandalize Michelle's car," she lied. "Your friend David did that, one time that I know of, and that was because he didn't want you with Michelle. Secondly, I love Michelle. Always have and always will. So no, I don't want her with you. And trust me, Michelle has made it quite clear that she's still in love with me. The only reason she married you was because she wanted a baby of her own and was afraid of what everyone would say if they knew about her being with a woman, since she was a relationship guru."

That time Calvin had the shocked look on his face. "She what?"

"You heard me right. We've been together since your so-called marriage. Yes, I was wrong with the rabbit thing, but she was wrong for trying to hide her pregnancy from me. And thankfully it drove her right into my arms and into the bed. I would have left it alone, but you decided to tear us apart altogether."

"You had sex with my wife?" Calvin asked as rage took over his once distraught expression.

"Newsflash! We were in a fucking relationship. And I do mean 'fucking.' She's gay just like you're gay. She doesn't need to be married to you. She and I could raise that baby together without your ass. Then you could have all the trannies that your heart can stand. You don't love her and I have all the proof I need. I will beg her for forgiveness and help her to understand why I did what I did, but you could never get Michelle to understand why you used her just to make partner so you could continue fucking a tran. You need to get over yourself, 'cause your goose is cooked," Angie said with confidence.

She was about to leave, but then turned back.

"Thanks for opening the door for me to reclaim my woman."

She went to pick up Michelle's pocketbook to take to her. Calvin pulled it. The pair tussled back and forth for the pocketbook.

"You are not taking my wife, my son, or this pocketbook," he said through gritted teeth.

"Watch me!" she responded as she continued to struggle for the pocketbook.

The pocketbook strap broke and all of the contents fell onto the floor. They both spotted the gun and then looked at each other.

30

David

"David! What are you doing here?"

"Is Calvin here?"

"No, I just left him in Tennessee. You know, in the house next to where you were videotaping." Michelle answered sarcastically, when opening the door to find David.

"Please, can I come in? I have to talk to you. I need to explain some things."

"I thought you were locked up or something."

"That's part of what I need to talk about. I just need for you to understand some things and get out of this marriage while you still can."

Michelle stared at him shivering in the cold for a moment. "Come in." David followed Michelle into the house, closing the door behind him. "To be quite honest, I'm not sure how I feel about what you did to my husband."

David didn't take her claim of 'my husband' as a good sign.

"Michelle, you need to get out of this house. Calvin is dangerous. He is so desperate for this partnership that he will say or do anything—"

"Like videotape him with a transsexual?" Michelle asked, cutting him off.

David threw his hands up. "Yes! Yes, I know I did that, but that was Angie's idea. She told me about the two of you being together and—"

Michelle almost stumbled where she stood from the shocking words. He caught hold of her and then continued.

"I'm sorry. Your secret is safe with me. But as I was saying, Angie only wanted you away from Calvin so the two of you could be together. She loves you. I never wanted to hurt anyone. I was doing quite fine taking the steps I needed to become partner. Calvin knew I had a good thing and tried to snatch my clients from me. The man went as far as threatening to kill me when we were in Chicago. The only reason I sent Angie the video was because I didn't know if Calvin would make good on his threat or not. If he did, at the very least, I wanted you to know what you're involved with so you and the baby could safely get away from him. Calvin is a desperate man. He even told me that he only married you and had to start a family so he could become partner. I even asked if he loved you and he said, 'This is business.' But after his last failed attempt to take me down, I know he means business and will do anything."

Michelle let the tears trickle down her face as she listened to David's cutting words.

"He sent that girl-man to my hotel room all beat up to claim I raped him. If it weren't for Angie telling my attorney to look at the hotel video, I'd still be locked up. They were able to see the guy had just shown up at my door and never entered my room. Apparently Calvin put a hurting on the guy real bad before sending him to my room."

"So what, now you want me to help you become a partner?"

David wrinkled his brow confused. "No! Not at all. They already told me the position was mine. It will be official next month."

"So they made you partner because of Calvin's indiscretions?"

"They made me a partner purely on my work abilities. They have no idea about Calvin's she-man. I didn't have to go there at all."

"So why the video? Why go through all of the trouble if you were not going to use it?"

"Like I said before, that was Angie's idea. I went along with it thinking it would score me points with Angie," David lied.

"Speaking of which, why did you lie and tell my husband that you were not seeing Angie after she clearly told me you were? What was the purpose behind that?"

"Michelle, I promise you, I have never been with Angie. I think she may have wanted you to think that because you would get jealous and get back with her," he answered convincingly.

Michelle went and took a seat as the plausibility made her legs weak. "Oh my goodness. It's like I don't even know her. Why would she go to such lengths?"

"I don't know. Sometimes love makes people do crazy things." He tried to smile.

"How long did you know my husband was gay?"

"When I saw that video. I knew that guy kept popping up whenever Calvin and I would be out, but I didn't know it was a man. I never got to see him close up and from a distance, he looked like a hot chick. All the guys would be checking him out. If only they knew. Angie mentioned at your wedding that he looked like a man. I laughed it off. Angie only expected to have proof that Calvin was cheating on you, period. I certainly didn't expect to see the extra surprise.

"To be quite honest with you, I'm not sure why Calvin pursued you. From the time I first laid eyes on you, I told him how beautiful you were and that I wanted to get to know you. He didn't show the slightest interest before then, and he was bothered by the fact that you wanted to meet him. Then I looked up and the two of you were getting married. I even tried talking him out of it because he made it clear that he had no love for you; only becoming partner."

"So why are you just now coming to me with all of this? Why didn't you come when you first saw my husband was fucking another man?"

"Do you remember how you treated me the last time I tried to warn you about him? Michelle, your husband is dangerous. That's why I'm here now. I am concerned about your safety. I want you to get out of here before he completely snaps and does something crazy to you and the baby. There's no telling what he'll do to you once he gets the official word that he won't be partner. That's all you ever were with him: a means to an end."

"Get out!" Michelle stood up and pointed toward the door. "Get the hell out!"

David looked at Michelle as if she'd gone mad. "Are you serious?"

"I said get out of my home. How dare you come and say those things? What, are you jealous because I chose to be with Calvin instead of you? Is that why you've been out to destroy him ever since? Is that why you drugged him and stole his belongings a few months ago? You needed to pay him back for deciding to be with me?"

"Michelle! Please listen to what I'm telling you. He will eat you and shit you out. I'm trying to save your life. This partnership was his whole life and now he doesn't have it and no longer has any need for you."

"That's what you know! Calvin told me that he was going to forfeit the partnership for me and he told me that other relationship is all over."

"He's lying to you. He's desperate. He'll tell you anything to ensure that you won't blow his chance to become partner—that is, until he finds out he won't be." David grabbed hold of Michelle's hands. "Please, I'm begging you, go grab some things and let me get you out of here to someplace safe."

Michelle screamed at the top of her lungs. "Get out of here! Leave me alone!" She continued to holler as if someone was killing her, while twisting from grasp.

"Michelle! Stop screaming. Okay, I'll go."

Then he turned to leave before he hit the floor seconds later.

31

Calvin

O h my goodness! Oh my goodness!" Michelle got down on her knees, shaking like a leaf, to see about David as his blood covered her hands. She looked up at Calvin standing at a distance holding her gun. When David held up his hand for help and coughed, Calvin walked up closer and shot him again until there was no breath left.

Michelle scooted away from where David's blood had spattered on her face. She shielded her face from Calvin with her arms as she boxed herself to a spot where she could no longer run. He stood over her before pulling her up by her arm.

"Oh my god, Calvin! Please . . . Please don't hurt me. I won't say a word. Please don't kill me and our baby," she pleaded.

"Are you sure that's my baby? Tony seems to think it's okay for you to come and sit your 'fat booty' on his lap. And Angie seems to have been getting off, sucking all in your pussy. What other secrets do you have? Were you fucking David too? Is that why I keep catching him in my house, trying to get you to leave me?"

Michelle was confused as well as terrified. "What are you talking about?"

Calvin chuckled. "It's funny that you were so quick to point fingers at me. I asked you to forgive me, but what I did was just unforgivable. And here

I catch you with my so-called best friend in my house. And by the way, your lesbian lover told me all about how she was in MY FUCKING PUSSY since you've been carrying my supposed baby."

"That's a lie! I have not!" Michelle yelled, momentarily forgetting her fear.

"But I don't care about that. I'm more concerned about this Tony. Wasn't that your ex-boyfriend or something?"

Michelle looked afraid. "Yes. He was long before you."

"And he's calling you now. Why? I listened to his corny-ass message on your voicemail. I heard him calling my fucking wife, 'Shelly-Poo,' and him telling you that if things don't work out, that you could always come and sit your fat ass on his lap and 'do what it do.' And I guess he wants to eat your pussy too, since he said he can still do the 'slurpee-slurpee' thing that you can't get enough of."

"Calvin, I swear I have not seen Tony since we broke up. He called me for the first time out of the blue the other day to warn me that his crazy wife was on a warpath and out to get me. He told me he's paralyzed because she shot him. I have not talked to him since then, nor before that. As for Angie, I have not been with Angie."

"You know, it's funny I believe you when you talk about that Tony character, but the minute you spoke about the lesbian, your convincing eyes suddenly shifted downwards. Why is that? Is there some truth to that lesbian bitch sucking my wife's pussy?" Calvin asked, raising his voice.

"Please, Calvin. You're scaring me."

"Then tell me the fucking truth! I want the truth now!" he demanded.

Michelle shuddered as she tried to move away from him, but he stayed close up on her.

"I'm sorry," she cried.

"I'm sorry? I'm sorry?" he laughed like a crazy man. "Funny, when I told you I was sorry, that didn't mean shit to you. But when you're sorry, that makes it all better."

"That was long ago when we were in college. I didn't want anyone to know I had been with a woman. I was confused back then."

"BULLSHIT! She came up to the mountain a little while ago and told me the two of you are still fucking, as recent as when your car was vandalized."

Michelle's scared eyes looked up confused. "That's a damn lie! I have not been with her. She's nothing more than a scorned woman. David just told me all the things she did because she wanted to be with me. I told her to stay away from me, even when she sent me the video of you and that man. We could call her here right now and you will see she is lying to you."

That time Calvin's eyes darted away. He walked away and put the gun down on the table, then took off his driving gloves. He sat down on the sofa and hung his head low. When he looked up again, Michelle's trembling hands were pointing the gun at him.

"You may as well pull the trigger. My life is over anyway. My wife doesn't want me. I don't have the partnership. I'll spend the rest of my life in jail because I killed the man I thought was attacking my wife."

"You thought he was attacking me? That's why you killed him?" she asked, turning the gun down.

"I heard screaming when I was pulling up to bring you your pocketbook and phone you left in the mountains. I saw him looking like he was coming at you, so I shot him." Calvin hung his head lower as he slumped over from the thought of his life falling apart.

Michelle put the gun down and went to sit next to him. She wrapped her arm around him. "I'm sorry, Calvin. This is all my fault. We'll just tell the police that David was trying to attack me and you walked in and caught him. They said he just raped somebody, so we could just tell them he was here to rape me," Michelle suggested. "They'll believe that. Surely they would not lock you up for that."

Calvin looked up into Michelle's eyes. He could hardly believe his ears. His wife was trying to find a way to help him. He sat up and leaned over to kiss her as if he loved her for the first time.

She pulled away after getting momentarily lost in his kiss. "There's a dead body in the middle of the floor."

"If I call the police, they'll think I killed him because he made partner and I didn't. They'll never believe he tried to hurt you."

Michelle frowned. "Well, what are we supposed to do then?"

"We're going to have to dispose of the body."

Michelle's eyes widened as she covered her mouth. "Can't we just call the police?" she cried.

"First they'll want to know why you didn't call right away. Then they will put us both on the front page of every newspaper before there's even a trial. Your whole lesbian lifestyle will come to the forefront and only God knows what else. Then what will that do to your mother and grandmother? We're going to have to handle this together. We have to work quickly. I want to get him out of here while we still have the night."

"My God, what have I done? My mother and grandmother would die."

"Well, that's why I need for you to be strong and help me with this."

When Michelle finished sobbing, yet again, she said, "Okay."

Calvin kissed her again before getting up to move the furniture so he could roll David's body up in the large Oriental rug. He instructed Michelle to bring David's car into the garage and she did so. Calvin loaded David's body into the trunk.

"Go get dressed and meet me up at the house in the mountains," he instructed. She was a nervous wreck. "Are you going to be okay to drive?" he calmly asked as if he killed for a living.

"No, I won't be okay! I've never done this before."

"Michelle, I need for you to get it together. I need for you to drive the other car, so you're going to have to calm down." He took her into his arms and held her tightly as she cried. When she seemed to have it together, he said, "Okay, baby, we have to get going. I'm going to go on now and I'll see you when you get up there. Call me if you have any problems. Just take a deep breath and you'll be fine."

Michelle got her nerves together and calmed down. Calvin kissed her forehead, grabbed his gloves, and left in David's car.

32

Michelle

When Calvin pulled off, she contemplated calling the police. She looked on the garage floor at the dark spots. When she touched it, she realized it was David's blood. She ran into the house to grab a bottle of bleach and poured it on the spots. Then she went into the front room where she saw his blood had seeped through the rug and cleaned that as well while she cried about the mess she had made from screaming unnecessarily.

"This is all my fault," she told herself.

She went to take a quick shower and noticed all of the blood splattered on her, which caused her to throw up. After getting herself cleaned up and putting her bloodstained clothes in a garbage bag, she went in the kitchen to call the housekeeper, who was scheduled to come that next morning, and asked her not to come. She didn't want anyone to start asking questions about the missing rug unless Calvin was there or he replaced it with a new one.

When she hung up the phone, the doorbell rang. All kinds of thoughts raced through her head. She looked around to make sure everything looked in order and then went to answer the door after she got herself together.

"May I help you?" she asked when she saw the attractive, well dressed woman on the other side of the door.

"Hi, my name is Talethia Jacqueford and I'm looking for David Mosley. He told me he was coming here and then he would be right back, but I haven't heard from him."

Michelle could feel the baby doing flip-flops around and grabbed her stomach as she hunched over. Talethia moved closer and put her hand on Michelle's back.

"Are you all right? Do you need to get to the hospital or something?"

"No, I'll be fine," Michelle answered excited. "I just need to sit down for a minute."

Talethia helped Michelle into the front room and could smell the bleach. "Do you think maybe the bleach could be getting to you? Pregnant women shouldn't use bleach, you know?"

"I know. I just hate dirt," she lied.

"Well, anyhow, have you seen David? He said he was coming here to warn you and I have not heard back from him. I was going to call the police, but I figured I better check with you first to see if you heard anything."

Michelle closed her eyes to avoid the piercing eyes of the woman who had all the makings of an attorney questioning a hostile witness on the stand.

Again Talethia asked, "Are you sure you're going to be all right? Do you need for me to get you some water or something?"

"I'll be fine. This happens all the time, but it goes away after a while. Really, I'll be okay. To answer your question, yes, David came here earlier, but I told him that my husband and I are separating, so he left."

"Didn't he tell you that you may be in danger?"

Michelle chuckled. "I'm not worried about anything."

"Is that why you leave a gun sitting out in the open like this?" Talethia pointed to the gun on the table.

Michelle's eyes shot over to the gun and then she nervously chuckled again. "Believe it or not, we have wild animals that roam the property. I get nervous sometimes. Especially at night. When I hear stuff outside, I'm not sure if it's the wind, an animal, or a burglar. So I keep it near." Michelle stood up to go pick up the gun from the table. "I'll take it back upstairs when you leave since I'll be going to bed."

"Isn't it kind of early for bed?" Talethia persisted.

Michelle was getting annoyed. "Look, what else do you want? I told you David is not here. I think you could leave now." Michelle started walking toward the door to escort her uninvited guest out.

"Well, here's my card. Please call me if you hear from him, or tell him to get in touch with me as soon as possible. I'll be waiting at his house and if he doesn't return by midnight, I'll have to call the police. Of course I will have to let them know this is the last place I knew he was at. They'll have their own set of questions for you."

Michelle had opened the door, but then slammed it closed before Talethia could leave. "What are you trying to imply here? Do you think I'm responsible for David's death?"

Talethia gasped. "David's death! Whoa! I never said that. I'm just simply trying to find the man, but I'll be leaving now. Who knows, he's probably at the house right now waiting for me." She managed a nervous smile.

Michelle's cell phone rang from the front room. She looked in its direction and then back at Talethia. She pointed the gun at her. "Move!" she commanded as she kept the barrel aimed in her direction while she made her way to her phone. She knew it had to be Calvin calling to check up on her and see if she was on the road.

When Michelle reached for the phone, Talethia tried to make a run for the door, but the bullet caught her in the back instead. Michelle dropped both the gun and the phone when she noticed Talethia hit the floor. Everything was going in slow motion before she finally collapsed.

When she came to, she was lying on the sofa with a wet towel over her forehead. As she tried to focus, she noticed Calvin moving about. Then she started thinking everything in her mind was just a bad dream.

"Oh, you're up?" he said as he came and sat beside her.

"What happened?" she grabbed her belly to be sure the baby was still in place.

Calvin kissed her head and rubbed the baby in her stomach. "The baby is fine and still moving around. When I called you, I didn't hear you say hello. I just heard a gunshot in the background so I rushed back home and found you lying on the floor. You must have passed out. Your phone and the gun were on the floor as well, next to you."

Michelle tried to sit up as she made heads or tails of her memory. "Gunshot? Who got shot?"

"I don't know who she was. If the business card next to you on the floor was hers, she's Talethia Jacqueford. Some attorney."

Michelle shifted back into panic mode and was on the verge of hyperventilating. "Oh my God! Where is she?"

"Don't worry, baby. I already took care of that, but we're going to have to get going so we could make it up to the mountain before it gets too late. Those roads will get too slick and icy at night. Or maybe you could just stay at the inn and come up and meet me in the morning. I don't want you staying here alone tonight. We can't have any more setbacks."

"I killed somebody?" Michelle asked, covering her mouth. "I'm a killer? Oh my lord, what have I done?"

"Who was she? Why was she here?" Calvin asked suspiciously.

"She was looking for David. She came here asking a lot of questions and said she was going to send the police here since this was the last known place he was going."

Calvin kissed her head again. "You did good, sweetie. Everything will work out just fine. Do you think you'll be okay to drive?"

Michelle held her head as she tried to get up. "I guess. I may need a few minutes."

"Okay, I'm going to get going. I'll call you in a little bit to make sure you're okay and on the road. Just check into the inn tonight and then ride up in the morning."

"All right." Michelle looked around and then asked, "Where is she?"

"With David. Don't worry. I'll take care of everything. And when you can, be sure to lock that gun up back upstairs in your closet."

"Okay." She stood up holding onto Calvin's hand as if her life depended on him. At that point, her life was in his hands.

He kissed her and then headed back out again. She looked around and aside from the missing rug, everything was in order. She was so thankful to have Calvin there to clean up her mess and come to her rescue. In that moment she made up her mind to forgive her husband for his indiscretions. At that point, she couldn't imagine her life without him.

After she locked the gun away, she packed a few clothes and then got on the long road ahead to Tennessee, where she checked into the "comfy" inn they stayed at before. She called Calvin repeatedly, but the call would go directly to his voicemail. Then she remembered that there was no phone signal up there where he was at.

33

Calvin

Calvin worked tirelessly through the night to get the two bodies cut up so he could burn them with the rise of the morning sun. He was still nervous about not cutting up Angie's body just the same. Instead, he threw her in the trunk of her rented car and parked it on a deserted road not too far from the inn. He figured it would be days before the car rental company would come searching for it, and by then all of his tracks would be covered.

Michelle showed up at nine that morning while the fires were still burning and the stench of blood was still in the air.

"Oh my god! Is that what I think it is?" she asked, trying to cover her nose.

"Michelle, go back to the inn and come back after noon," he said, trying to shield her from the sight.

"I tried calling you over and over to see what time I should come, but you don't have a signal." Just then, Michelle vomited from the horrible odor.

"Honey, just go back down there. I'll walk down there and meet you later. Also, I need for you to tell them you'll be there for a couple more nights. I don't think it would be good for you to go back to the house just yet. I still have to get that other car out of there and make sure everything is cleaned up."

"Calvin," Michelle said with disappointment, "I'm scared."

"I know you are, baby. That's why it's best for you to stay at the inn until all the smoke clears. Let me get everything all cleaned up. At least I'll be able to reach you there by phone."

"Fine. I need to go inside to use the bathroom and rinse this taste from my mouth. The baby is pressing on my bladder. Plus, I think I'm going to throw up again," she said as she rushed inside while trying to cover her nose and mouth.

"Go ahead, and do me a favor and bring me that gas can when you return. It's near the fireplace," he yelled out.

"Is this Angie's wallet that I just found in the fireplace?" she asked when returning with the gas can.

Calvin closed his eyes and then reopened them to look at a stunned Michelle. "Baby, you have to understand, she was trying to destroy us. You said yourself that she was doing bad things to you."

Michelle was about to run away to the car, but Calvin caught up with her and hugged her. "Honey, I know this looks bad, but she came here yesterday after you left and said she wanted everyone to know about you and her and that you were going to take our baby and raise him with her. She tried to grab your pocketbook, accusing me of doing something to harm you, and when your gun fell out, she went to grab it to shoot me. I had to defend myself. I swear," Calvin said, stretching the truth.

The truth was that he grabbed the gun first and made Angie plead for her life before shooting her in the back of the head while she was on her knees. Since he was in a rush to go confront Michelle about her infidelity, he hadn't taken the time to dispose of Angie's body in the manner he did the others.

"How many? How many others are there, Calvin? How many people are now dead? Are you going to kill me and the baby too?" she yelled through tears, hitting him in the chest before resting her head against it.

He held her tight and kissed the top of her head. "Baby, I know this is difficult, but we'll get through this together. We could move away someplace and get a fresh start."

"How do I move away from the memories? Do you have an answer for that? How do I just pretend I didn't kill someone or that my best friend is dead because she was in love with me? What about her son? Who's going to raise that child? And how do I forget that my foolish screaming caused an innocent man to be killed?"

"Honey, I know this is not easy. I have to live with it too. We'll live it together. Just you, me, and our son when he gets here. Right now, I need you to go back to the hotel and stay put." Calvin walked Michelle back to the car. "Everything will be all right. It's just going to take some time."

Michelle got in the car and left without saying anything else. It made Calvin uneasy.

The following day Calvin showed up to his office expecting to clear out his belongings.

"Mr. Edwards, the partners have been trying to reach you. They asked that you come to see them immediately. Should I let them know you're here now?" Calvin's secretary asked.

Calvin already anticipated them grilling him about the whole Julissa fiasco. "That's fine. Let me know when they're ready."

Calvin sat in his office for about an hour, blankly staring out the window as his world was crumbling.

"They're ready to see you now," she buzzed into his intercom.

"Thanks."

He took the long walk up to the conference room, feeling like it was a walk to the electric chair he'd face if his deeds were ever revealed. He was glad to see only two of the senior partners waiting in the conference room, versus the whole firing squad.

"Hey, Calvin. Have a seat," Mr. Pugh instructed.

Calvin took the hot seat in silence and exchanged a phony smile with the other senior partner, Mr. Whitmore.

"How's the wife and baby doing? We were a little concerned," Mr. Pugh asked.

At first, Calvin forgot the lie that he told them, but he quickly remembered. "Oh, she's doing much better now. She was having mild contractions, but the doctor said it was normal for some," he lied.

"Oh, how I remember those days," Mr. Whitmore chimed in. "I remember my wife going through that with all four of our children. Thankfully, those days are done."

"I seem to remember a few scares with my wife as well." Mr. Pugh chuckled and then shifted into business mode. "But anyhow, we want to get right to the point. As you know, it's been a long, tough road for the partner opening, and while you have been quite an outstanding candidate, our choice was unanimously David Mosley. However, he seems to have run into a bit of legal trouble while in Chicago and although his attorney assured us that the matter was some type of frame up, we've decided to go with the runner up since we can't seem to reach David at this point."

Calvin's eyes were focused on a small chip in the large Brazilian cherry wood conference table. His eyes immediately sprung up when he realized he was the runner up. "Me?" he asked, trying to contain his excitement as he looked back and forth at each partner.

"Yes, you. That is, if you're still interested," Mr. Whitmore answered.

Calvin stood up and ran to shake both men's hands. He could hardly believe it.

"We believe in you, Calvin, so don't let us down," Mr. Pugh told him as he shook Calvin's hands. "Now take the rest of the day off so you can go celebrate with the little lady. It's going to get really busy in the weeks ahead while we get this process going."

Calvin laughed with excitement. "Oh, you won't be disappointed. You have no idea how much this means to me."

Calvin left the office and decided to check on things at the condo before going to see about his wife and share the good news. The security guard on duty called out to Calvin as he was about to rush by.

"Mr. Edwards!"

Calvin turned back. "Hey Joe! How's it going?" Then he noticed the glum look on Joe's face. "What's the matter?"

"I think you better take a look at this," he said, handing Calvin the DVD left with the other security guard a few days prior. "A woman came by saying she was your wife and left it. We were going to give it to Mrs. Edwards, but we haven't seen her for a few days. I think the two women may have collided. They said she looked in pretty bad shape when she was here."

Calvin took the video, confused. "Who was in bad shape and who left this video saying they were my wife?"

"The lady from the talk show came and said she was your wife. I think her name is Michelle Post. They said she was a petite sized woman. Your wife— Julissa was in bad shape. No one has seen her since that day."

Calvin covered his mouth to contain his flaring temper. "Thanks, Joe. I'll look into it. I just got back from a business trip and hadn't had a chance to call and check on her."

Joe smiled a distressed smile, since he had already watched the video.

Calvin went up to his condo and released his anger before popping the DVD in and becoming angry all over again. He knew then he would make Michelle pay dearly, since it was obvious by Joe's expression that he and everyone else had watched the video.

34

Michelle

After three days of not hearing from Calvin, Michelle decided to return home. There was no sign of Calvin and it looked as if most of his clothes were gone along with the luggage set that was missing from the garage. She did see a new rug down on the floor that replaced the previous rug. She smiled at Calvin's thoughtfulness, but then got closer as she smelled a familiar fragrance coming from it. It smelled like Julissa. When Michelle kneeled down, she even noticed Julissa's hair scattered on it.

She was fuming. *How dare he bring a rug from that other woman?* she thought. She got into her car and drove to the condo and was stopped by a different security officer.

"Where the fuck is he at? Tell him his wife is here."

"Ma'am, you're going to have to vacate the premises before I have you locked up for trespassing."

"How are you going to have me locked up for trespassing when this is my husband's home?" she asked smugly.

"Well, you need to take that up with him when you see him. In the meantime, you need to leave here, now."

"Yeah, okay. Just let him know I got something for his ass. He can't hide forever," she said, storming out into the cold night.

Michelle returned to the house to find several police cars there. She was gripped with fear, not knowing why they were there. She wondered if something had happened to Calvin while she was behaving poorly.

"Michelle Post-Edwards?" an officer asked as she approached the opened door.

"Yes. Is my husband in there? Did something happen to him?"

They quickly spun her around and placed handcuffs on her as they read her Miranda rights to her.

"What the hell is going on? What are you doing?" she yelled.

"You are under arrest for the murder of John Winters."

"Who? John Winters? I don't know any John Winters. You're making a big mistake."

"John Winters, aka Julissa Winters. We found her head in the trash bag you threw in the dump, along with the bullet you left in her head. We found your gun in the closet, and our lab is checking for a match. We found a bag with your clothes stained with blood as well as a lot of bleach stains. It's apparent that you've been doing some housekeeping of a murder scene. Also, we have officers en route to Tennessee to check the area where you've been hiding out for the past few days."

"I was not hiding out. I was there waiting for my husband."

"Interesting. Go on," the police captain encouraged. Michelle sobbed and then yelled, "I didn't touch that beast! She's the one who came here traumatizing me and then went off to go fuck my husband."

"Oh really? Funny, your husband filed a missing person report when she hadn't shown back up at her home for several days. And rom the look of your husband's closet, it seems he has moved out. I take it you two were separated?"

Before Michelle could respond, a CSI came out from the house.

"Captain, could you come in here? We found cleaned blood in three places and two drains," the crime scene investigator said.

Michelle could feel a rush of blood in her head as she was escorted to a squad car. She wanted to know where Calvin was and needed for him to explain the misunderstanding. Then she thought about the captain saying something about a head in a trash bag with her fingerprints. When she saw what she thought was a dead animal in the bag, she placed it in the trash container to go out with the rest of the garbage. She had no idea any head was in the bag. The biggest problem was, no one ever took the garbage cans to the curb to be picked up on garbage day. Although it was obvious that Calvin had been back to the house, he didn't touch the garbage cans.

She also couldn't help but feel that somehow her husband set her up to take the fall for all of the murders. She had no idea that his lover was also murdered. Her mind thought back to the day she found Calvin up at the mountain house with the intention of killing him and his lover. Now it all made sense how he confidently assured her that Julissa would never be a problem again. As her mind tried to piece everything together, it became obvious to Michelle that Calvin used her gun to kill his lover. He must have cut her body up in pieces and taken the remnants to Tennessee where she found him. Her mind flashed back to the fact that Calvin wore gloves every time. He had on gloves when he brought the gun into the house. He had on gloves when he had her go in the Tennessee house for the gas can. He had on gloves when he was cleaning up her mess behind the attorney. He wore gloves as if he was a professional hit man.

"You sneaky bastard!" Michelle yelled out from the back of the squad car as she pieced everything together. She thought for certain the police would easily see none of it could have been her, especially in her condition, but the more they asked questions, the more she seemed to incriminate herself.

The following morning, after sitting in the interrogation room all night, Michelle was formerly charged with four murders and the FBI was taking over the case because of the interstate jurisdiction. She was glad when someone let her know her husband was waiting outside with an attorney. However, when the bumbling idiot of an attorney came into the room, she knew she was doomed. Calvin obviously went out and found the most incompetent lawyer in the yellow pages. She was not allowed to see Calvin and couldn't understand why.

Her hostile temper toward her attorney hurt her even more when officers had to run and restrain her when she started to attack the lawyer, who kept twisting up all of her words. She got word back to Calvin that she needed a new lawyer. Another day passed before yet another incompetent attorney showed up for her arraignment, where her bail was denied and she was shipped off to the women's detention facility to await her trial set for almost a year later.

When she was finally able to get a visit with Calvin, he acted as if he was more distraught than she.

"They said you moved out and that we separated. Why?" Michelle asked.

Calvin hid his anger and told her through the thick Plexiglas, "Michelle, I didn't want anything to happen to the baby, and you just seemed like I was causing you so much stress."

Michelle looked at him confused, "I should have just called the police when—"

"You need to be careful of what you say on here because they monitor all of your conversations. I don't want you to say anything that's going to make things worse. Please just keep quiet in here. You're going to only hurt your case," Calvin cut her off to warn.

"But—" Michelle started.

Calvin put his finger over his lips. "Shh. I love you. We'll find a new lawyer and get you out of here. You just have to watch what you say around here."

That was easy for him to say, Michelle thought as the tears flowed from her eyes.

Calvin blew a teary-eyed kiss to her as he made a quick escape while Michelle watched him looking as if he was really distraught about her position. And that was enough for her to have full faith in her husband.

35

Calvin

Two months later, Calvin was at the hospital to take custody of his new son, Calvin Jr. Michelle looked like she had already died but was still existing.

Unbeknownst to Michelle, Calvin saw to it that Michelle would be tied to all murders and had no way of justifying a thing. Originally, he didn't set out to hang her, but he was always mindful that he needed to cover his own tracks just in case anyone ever came looking. He felt Julissa, David, and the lawyer were all Michelle's fault. He was all too happy to put Angie out of her meddling misery. He also felt it was Michelle's fault for putting Julissa's head in the garbage and for trying to out his desire to be with transsexuals to the security guard at his condo, forcing him to have to file a missing persons report.

After learning she gave the DVD to his condo security to hurt him, he took the rug from the condo and placed it in the house since he knew there would be plenty of Julissa's hair on it. But even before then, he left more than enough evidence to show Michelle was at the house in the mountains. When Michelle picked up Angie's wallet from the fireplace with her bare hands, he didn't bother to burn it. He didn't touch the gas can he had her bring outside after Michelle placed her prints on it. He also left the remnants of her vomit outdoors and in the toilet that didn't flush completely. He was sure to make Michelle touch the gun last, all just in case anyone ever came looking. By filing the missing persons report, he led police to his condo, where the security gave damaging statements about her state of mind and behavior while there.

By the time she started getting fed up with prison life, she attempted to throw Calvin under the bus, but there wasn't a soul who believed her. Her own attorney decided to go with the insanity defense, as that seemed like the only hope she possessed.

Calvin's new partners were very empathetic as he put on the façade of being the devastated victim of his wife's actions while putting his best foot forward to earn the company big dollars. Little did they know, while they were giving him some time off to help deal with his grief and his wife's legal issues that they didn't want to come back and haunt them, Calvin was finding comfort elsewhere.

He found Natalia about a week after Michelle's arrest at the same club where he met Julissa. By the time the baby was born, he allowed his new lover to move into the home to work as his nanny during business hours. She seemed to have natural maternal instincts and took excellent care of Calvin, Jr. He liked that Natalia was more beautiful than Julissa, two years younger, and came with a larger package than Julissa. Even better, Natalia didn't have the slightest bit of huskiness in her voice, nor any manly features that could be seen outside of the bedroom. His own family couldn't tell Natalia was born as Nathan. She was very submissive and didn't have anywhere near the bad and unpredictable attitude that Julissa possessed. When he returned to work, he'd even have his sexy nanny bring his son by the office on occasion to show off his baby boy. Even the partners were egging him on to be sure to "bone his gorgeous nanny" because they figured his marriage was pretty much over, as he put on the façade that he was still grieving over his wife's actions and wasn't sure he could trust again. Little did they know.

Since he didn't have to worry about his partners, Calvin had no problem being seen in public with Natalia and his son, while leaving Michelle to rot away in prison for a lifetime. The news had labeled her "A Scorned Woman" when they got wind of her affair with Angie. They put their own spin on the story by suggesting that Michelle murdered Angie because she rejected Michelle to be with David. They decided that she killed Julissa (Calvin's "superstar model" client) out of insecurity. The news of her deceased sister was attached to her, also being a murderer. Michelle's request of a speedy trial, with the hopes of being released sooner, only sped up the guarantee that she would receive a lethal injection sooner than later. She was found guilty on all charges. Her insanity defense was rejected.

Calvin didn't want to chance visiting Michelle and her trying to speak with him about the crimes. However, out of guilt, he would frequently send her pictures of the baby, but he wouldn't dare take his son in that environment. He felt sending pictures was the least he could do as he continued living his best life.

The End

NOTE FROM THE AUTHOR

Thank you for reading *A Scorned Woman*. When you're all done, be sure to leave a review and let others know how much you've enjoyed the story. No spoilers! If you enjoyed this book, be sure to check out:

9ine of Fools
Tapioca Pudding Next Door
Trapped in the Closet
Superwoman

Between Sisters
Between More Sisters
Caught Up Between Sisters
The Evolution Between Sisters
Revenge Between Sisters
Sister's Daughter
Never Again Between Sisters

NOTE: Tapioca Pudding's sequel is in *Never Again Between Sisters (of the Between Sisters series).*

To find out what other books Queendom Dreams will be releasing and other authors with Queendom Dreams Publishing, please visit us online at www.queendomdreamspublishing.com.

Queendom Dreams

ABOUT THE QUEEN

The Queen has been writing for many years, ranging in short stories, poetry, plays, professional and other writings. She is a native of (Queensbridge) Long Island City, New York. Her debut novel was *Between Sisters* (of the Between Sisters series). Her education includes Business and International Business Administration, as well as Travel & Tourism. When she's not writing, she loves to travel to sunny climates with clear and turquoise waters or near mountains for inspiration.

CPSIA information can be obtained
at www.ICGtesting.com
Printed in the USA
BVHW031638050919
557692BV00001B/49/P

9 781733 644211